THE
LITTLE
BOOK
OF
GREAT
BRITAIN

NEIL R. STOREY

The
History
Press

In memory of Theo,
a Great Briton.

First published 2012

The History Press
The Mill, Brimscombe Port
Stroud, Gloucestershire, GL5 2QG
www.thehistorypress.co.uk

© Neil R. Storey, 2012

The right of Neil R. Storey to be identified as the Author
of this work has been asserted in accordance with the
Copyrights, Designs and Patents Act 1988.

British Library Cataloguing in Publication Data.
A catalogue record for this book is available from the British Library.

ISBN 978 0 7524 7114 3

Typesetting and origination by The History Press
Printed in Great Britain

CONTENTS

	Introduction	5
1.	Topography & Around Britain	7
2.	Battles & Wars	23
3.	Royalty	44
4.	Great Britons – Famous & Not So Famous	50
5.	Britain at Work	59
6.	That's Entertainment	63
7.	Food & Drink	83
8.	Legends, Ghosts & Curiosities	94
9.	Transport	106
10.	Natural History	118
11.	Sports Roundup	126
12.	Sense of Place – Quintessentially British	138
13.	On this Day	159
	Acknowledgements	192

INTRODUCTION

The British are a unique race because much of their lives, work and leisure are inextricably entwined with Britain's history, scenery, celebrations, traditions and love of nostalgia that endows them with their own very distinctive identity and sense of place.

Visitors to these shores can only obtain some impression of the country and its character but how many people really know Britain, even if it is the country they call home? Despite being a small island there is always something new to discover, be it fascinating, frivolous, quirky or even bizarre. This book does not pretend to be a history, concise almanac or guide to Great Britain, instead it is a celebration of Britishness through a host of topics that explore the more eccentric and eclectic people and things that contribute to and define Great Britain; indeed, this book is a collection of the ephemeral and miscellaneous facts about this land you didn't know you wanted to know . . . until now. The contents of this volume will enliven conversation or quiz and leave even those who know and love Britain with the 'well fancy that!' factor. Things like . . .

Queen Elizabeth I (1533–1603) was the first British monarch to have a fully fitted flushing toilet.

A saggar maker's bottom knocker was a real job in the British pottery industry.

Biggles creator Captain W.E. Johns began his professional life as an assistant sanitary inspector.

There are over 470 recipes and flavours for British sausages and 1,200 varieties of native British apples.

The first person to be convicted of speeding is believed to be Walter Arnold of East Peckham, Kent, who on 28 January 1896, was fined 1*s* plus costs for driving at 8mph.

The Green Cross Code man and the helmeted figure of Darth Vader in *Star Wars* were both played by British muscle man David Prowse.

There are 19,500 bus stops in London.

The first World Conker Championships were staged at Ashton, Northamptonshire, in 1965.

The oldest continually held race has been held at Carnwath in Lanarkshire, Scotland since 1508 and still maintains the same prize for the winner – a pair of hand-knitted knee-length socks.

And my personal favourite . . .

Ian Fleming, the creator of 007 James Bond, was also the author of children's favourite *Chitty Chitty Bang Bang*.

You will soon see the ease with which one can enliven conversation, impress and intrigue family with the facts and frivolities obtained from this book.

1

TOPOGRAPHY &
AROUND BRITAIN

ABOUT BRITAIN

Great Britain was created by the Acts of Union between the Kingdom of England and Wales and the Kingdom of Scotland on 1 May 1707, and the twin Acts that united the Kingdom of Great Britain and the Kingdom of Ireland were passed respectively on 2 July 1800 and 1 August 1800 to create the United Kingdom of Great Britain and Ireland that came into effect on 1 January 1801.

The total area of the United Kingdom is approximately 94,060sq miles.

The coastline of Great Britain stretches for 11,073 miles and there is no location in Britain that is more than 74½ miles from the sea.

The highest point in Great Britain is the summit of Ben Nevis in Scotland which soars skywards to 4,406ft.

The lowest point in Great Britain is to be found at Holme Fen in Cambridgeshire at around 9ft below sea level.

The oldest rocks in the British Isles are the Lewisian gneisses, metamorphic rocks found in the far north-west of Scotland and in the Hebrides (with a few small outcrops elsewhere), which date from at least 2,700 million years ago.

During the Anglian Glaciation, about 478,000 to 424,000 years ago, ice up to 3,300ft thick reached as far south as London and Bristol and diverted the River Thames to its present course.

The prevailing wind across Great Britain is from the south-west.

The Wash is the largest estuarine system in the United Kingdom and contains England's largest official nature reserve. Providing an internationally important habitat for fifteen species of birds, it is home for 6,000 common seals and harbours a tenth of Britain's saltmarsh.

CANONICAL LATIN NAMES FOR THE ANCIENT REGIONS OF BRITAIN

Albion or Britannia (Britain)
Anglia (England)
Caledonia (Scotland)
Cambria (Wales)
Cornubia (Cornwall)
Hibernia (Ireland)
Scotia (originally the Roman name for Ireland). The name shifted in the Middle Ages to designate the part of Britain lying north of the Firth of Forth (the Kingdom of Alba). By the later Middle Ages it had become the fixed Latin term for what in English is called Scotland.

Ancient England and Wales had its capital at Winchester and in Westminster after the Norman Conquest of 1066, and consisted of the kingdoms of Wessex, Mercia, East Anglia, Northumbria, Cornwall and the Principality of Wales.

Telly Savalas, famous for his appearances in the American TV cop show *Kojak* in the 1970s, made three fifteen-minute British travelogue and tourism films entitled: *Telly Savalas Looks at Aberdeen* (1981), *Telly Savalas Looks at Portsmouth* (1981), and *Telly Savalas Looks at Birmingham* (1981). Telly speaks with confidence about the history, notable features and events he saw in each location (although he did not visit any of the locations during the filming) and concluded with a special variation of one of his popular catchphrases: 'So long Portsmouth, Here's looking at you'; 'So long Aberdeen, Here's looking at you' and my personal favourite where Telly remarks candidly: 'Yes, it's my kind o' town, so, so long Birmingham, here's looking at you.'

The remarkable Telly Savalas trilogy was followed by the series *Pete Murray takes you to . . .* where the popular DJ and regular *Juke Box Jury* panellist (1959–67), guided audiences around Nottingham (1982), Hastings (1982) and Coventry (1983).

EXTREMITIES

Although the extremities of Great Britain are often claimed as John O'Groats in Scotland and Land's End in the south, the northernmost point in Britain is in fact Dunnet Head (also known as Easter Head) in Caithness, Scotland, while the most southernmost point is The Lizard in Cornwall. The most westerly point of the mainland of Great Britain is at West Ardnamurchan in the highlands of Scotland and the furthest point east is to be found at Lowestoft Ness in Suffolk.

THE CENTRE OF BRITAIN

A number of locations have claimed to be the centre of Great Britain. The stone cross at Meriden in the West Midlands was claimed to be the centre for centuries. The claim for the centre of Britain was also made for the Midland Oak on the boundaries of Lillington and Leamington Spa in Warwickshire and Haltwhistle in Northumberland. Using modern methods of mapping using global positioning system (GPS), according to Ordnance Survey, the centre of mainland Great Britain is at grid reference SD 723 367 (3.4 miles south-west of Clitheroe, between Whalley, Billington and Calderstones Hospital in Lancashire). To be precise SD 72321 36671 to the nearest metre.

THE FIVE SMALLEST
CITIES IN GREAT BRITAIN

St David's, Pembrokeshire, Wales	pop. 1,797
St Asaph, Denbighshire, Wales	pop. 3,491
City of London, London, England	pop. 7,185
Wells, Somerset, England	pop. 10,406
Bangor, Gwynedd, Wales	pop. 13,725

THE HISTORIC COUNTIES OF ENGLAND

Bedfordshire
Berkshire
Buckinghamshire
Cambridgeshire
Cheshire
Cornwall
Cumberland
Derbyshire
Devon
Dorset
Durham
Essex
Gloucestershire
Hampshire
Herefordshire
Hertfordshire
Huntingdonshire
Kent
Lancashire
Leicestershire
Lincolnshire
Middlesex
Monmouthshire
Norfolk
Northamptonshire
Northumberland
Nottinghamshire
Oxfordshire
Rutland
Shropshire
Somerset
Staffordshire
Suffolk
Surrey
Sussex
Warwickshire
Westmorland
Wiltshire
Worcestershire
East Riding of Yorkshire
North Riding of Yorkshire
West Riding of Yorkshire

THE HISTORIC COUNTIES OF WALES

Anglesey
Brecknockshire
Carmarthenshire
Caernarvonshire
Cardiganshire
Denbighshire
Flintshire
Glamorganshire
Merionethshire
Monmouthshire
Montgomeryshire
Pembrokeshire
Radnorshire

THE HISTORIC COUNTIES OF SCOTLAND

Aberdeenshire
Angus (Forfarshire)
County of Argyll
Ayrshire
Banffshire
Berwickshire
County of Bute
Caithness
Clackmannanshire
Cromartyshire
Dumfriesshire
Dunbartonshire
County of Edinburgh (Midlothian)
County of Fife
Haddingtonshire (East Lothian)
Inverness-shire
Kincardineshire

Kinross-shire
Kirkcudbrightshire
Lanarkshire
Elgin (County of Moray)
Nairnshire
Orkney
Peeblesshire
Perthshire
Renfrewshire
Ross-shire
Roxburghshire
Selkirkshire
Stirlingshire
Sutherland
Linlithgowshire (West Lothian)
Wigtownshire
Zetland (Shetland)

NATIONAL PARKS

Great Britain has fifteen National Parks, namely (and the year of their designation):

The Brecon Beacons (1957)
The Broads (1989)
The Cairngorms (2003)
Dartmoor (1951)
Exmoor (1954)
The Lake District (1951)
Loch Lomond and the Trossachs (2002)
The New Forest (2005)
Northumberland (1956)
North York Moors (1952)
Peak District (1951)
Pembrokeshire Coast (1952)
Snowdonia (1951)
South Downs (2010)
Yorkshire Dales (1954)

LAND AREA COVERED BY NATIONAL PARKS

England: 10 National Parks cover 9.3 per cent of the land area
Wales: 3 National Parks cover 19.9 per cent of the land area
Scotland: 2 National Parks cover 7.2 per cent of the land area

The Lake District is England's largest National Park. It covers 885 square miles with a width (west to east) of 33 miles and 40 miles (north to south). The deepest lake is Wastwater at 243ft, the longest lake is Windermere which is 10½ miles long. To be precise there is only one official lake in the Lake District – Bassenthwaite Lake – all the others are 'meres' or 'waters'.

Britain's largest National Park is the Cairngorms, which covers an area of 1,748 sq miles, over twice the size of the Lake District and Loch Lomond and the Trossachs. Five of Scotland's six highest mountains are within the park, and there are 55 summits over 2,900ft. 36 per cent of the land area is over 2,600ft and 2 per cent is over 3,000ft. The land above 1,900ft is known as the 'montane zone' and is the largest area of arctic mountain landscape in the British Isles.

TWENTY THREE-LETTER PLACE NAMES IN BRITAIN

Ayr (Ayrshire)
Ely (Cambridgeshire)
Esh (Durham)
Eye (Suffolk)
Ham (Kent)
Hoe (Norfolk)
How (Cumbria)
Ide (Devon)
Kea (Cornwall)
Lag (Dumfriesshire)

Lee (Lancashire)
Lew (Oxfordshire)
Nox (Shropshire)
Ore (West Sussex)
Par (Cornwall)
Raw (North Yorkshire)
Rhu (Dunbartonshire)
Rye (East Sussex)
Usk (Gwent)
Wem (Shropshire)

REALLY ANCIENT BRITONS

In July 2010 archaeologists digging near the village of Happisburgh in Norfolk discovered seventy-eight pieces of razor-sharp flint shaped into primitive cutting and piercing tools believed to have been laid down by hunter-gatherers of the human species *Homo antecessor* otherwise known as 'Pioneer Man' some 840,000–950,000 years ago. This makes them the oldest human artefacts ever found in Britain and the earliest known *Homo* genus in Northern Europe.

Other early human remains found in Britain include *Homo heidelbergensis*, 'Boxgrove Man', who existed 478,000–524,000 years ago and *Homo neanderthalensis*, 'Neanderthal Man' of 230,000 years ago.

POPULATION

The population of mainland Great Britain since 1801:

1801	10,942,646
1811	11,964,303
1821	14,091,757
1831	16,261,183
1841	18,534,332
1851	20,816,351
1861	23,128,518
1871	26,072,284
1881	29,710,012

1891	33,028,172
1911	40,831,396

(United Kingdom of Great Britain and Ireland)

1921	42,769,196
1931	46,038,000
1951	50,225,000
1961	52,589,000
1971	55,780,000
1981	56,343,000
1991	57,338,000
2001	58,789,000
2011	62,262,000

The UK population continues to age gradually. The number of people aged 85 and over was more than 1.4 million in mid-2011, comprising 460,000 men and 951,000 women, and accounting for 2.3 per cent of the total population. Between 1981 and 2011, this age group increased by just over 0.8 million.

In mid-2011, there were more people of state pensionable age than there were under-16s.

SOME OF BRITAIN'S LARGEST CITY DISTRICTS WITH THEIR POPULATIONS

(Reported as the 2010 mid-year estimates from the Office for National Statistics)

Greater London	7,172,091
Birmingham	1,036,900
Leeds	798,800
Sheffield	555,500
City of Glasgow	592,800
City of Edinburgh	486,100
Bradford	512,600
Manchester	498,800
Liverpool	445,200
Coventry	315,700

WHAT'S IN A NAME?

In 1841 the returns of the census revealed the most popular girls' names were Mary (1.43m) and Elizabeth (809,000); for boys it was John (1.28m) and William (1m) – a top four that remained unchanged for 50 years.

According to the Office for National Statistics the ten most popular names for baby girls 2011/12 are:

Olivia	Ruby
Lily	Chloe
Sophie	Amelia
Jessica	Grace
Emily	Mia

And for baby boys:

Oliver	Alfie
Jack	William
Harry	James
Charlie	Joshua
Thomas	George

TEN OF THE OLDEST SIGNIFICANT REMAINS OF BUILDINGS IN GREAT BRITAIN

Knap of Howar, Orkney – A Neolithic farmstead dating from 3500 BC
Jarlshof, Shetland –A complex of wheelhouses dating from 200 BC
Temple of Claudius – Colchester, Essex, about AD 60
Caerleon Roman Amphitheatre – Monmouthshire, about AD 90
Painted House – Dover, Kent, about AD 200
Beehive cells – Eileach an Naoimh, Argyll, *c.* 6th century AD
St Martin's Church – Canterbury, Kent, AD 597
Church of St Peter-on-the-Wall – Bradwell, Essex, AD 654
Escomb Church – County Durham, about AD 670
The Crypt of Ripon Cathedral, Ripon, Yorkshire, AD 672

THE HOUSE OF GOD

Liverpool Cathedral is the largest Anglican cathedral and church in Europe.

Salisbury Cathedral has the tallest extant church spire in the United Kingdom that stands a lofty 404ft tall. The second tallest spire is that of Norwich Cathedral at 315ft.

The tallest spire ever constructed on a British church was built on Lincoln Cathedral and completed in 1311. It stood 524ft making it the tallest spire in the world until its collapse during a storm in 1549.

SOME ECCENTRIC BRITISH PLACE NAMES

Assloss, Kilmarnock, East Ayrshire
Bell End, near Bromsgrove, Worcestershire
Blue Vein, near Box, Wiltshire
Boghead, near Tarland, Aberdeenshire
Bottom Flash, (a lake) near Winsford, Cheshire
Bottom, Mossley, Greater Manchester
Botusfleming, near Saltash, Cornwall
Brown Willy, Bodmin Moor, Cornwall
Bully Hole Bottom, near Gaerllwyd, Monmouthshire
Buttock, near Barley, Lancashire
Cess, Martham, Norfolk
Crackpot, Swaledale, North Yorkshire
Curry Mallet, near Taunton, Somerset
Dirt Pot, Allendale, Northumberland
Dog Village, near Exeter
Donkey Town, near Camberley, Surrey
Diggle, east of Oldham, Greater Manchester
Durdle Door, near West Lulworth, Dorset
Fingringhoe, near Colchester, Essex
Fustyweed, Lyng, Norfolk
Golden Balls, near Clifton Hampden, Oxfordshire
Great Snoring, near Walsingham, Norfolk
Haseley Knob, near Kenilworth, Warwickshire
Helions Bumpstead, near Saffron Walden, Essex
Hole in the Wall, near Ross-on-Wye, Herefordshire
Knockdown, near Malmsbury, Wiltshire
Land of Nod, near Grayshott, Hampshire
Loggerheads, between Stoke and Shrewsbury (also another near Mold)

Lumps of Garryhorn, near Carsphairn, Dumfries and Galloway
Messing, near Colchester, Essex
Mucking, near Tilbury, Essex
Nempnett Thrubwell, south of Bristol
Nether Wallop, near Andover
North Piddle, Worcestershire
Oh Me Edge, near Byreness, Northumberland
Old Sodbury, Gloucestershire
Pant, near Oswestry, Shropshire
Plucks Gutter, near Ramsgate, Kent
Pratt's Bottom, near Farnborough
Prickwillow, Cambridgeshire
Raw, near Whitby
Scratby, Norfolk
Scratchy Bottom, near Durdle Door, Dorset
Shingay cum Wendy, Cambridgeshire
Slack Bottom, near Hebden Bridge, West Yorkshire
Splott, Cardiff
Steeple Bumpstead, near Haverhill, Essex
Throcking, near Stevenage, Hertfordshire
Thrupp, near Stroud
Thwing, near Bridlington
Tincleton, near Dorchester, Dorset
Tiltups End, near Nailsworth, Gloucestershire
Tomtit's Bottom, near Cowley, south of Cheltenham, Gloucestershire
Turner's Puddle, near Dorchester, Dorset
Ugley, near Bishop's Stortford, Essex
Undy, near Caldicot, Monmouthshire
Zeal Monachorum, north-west of Exeter

BRITISH PLACE NAMES THAT MAKE YOU THINK TWICE

Booby Dingle, Peterchurch, Herefordshire
Bumwell Hill, Carleton Rode, Norfolk
Bushy Bottom, Edburton, West Sussex
Bushygap, Northumberland
Cock Play, Bewcastle, Cumbria
Cockintake, Staffordshire
Cocklick End, near Slaidburn, Lancashire
Crapstone, near Plymouth, Devon
Droop, near Dorchester
Great Cockup, near Bassenthwaite, Cumbria

Lickey End, near Bromsgrove, Worcestershire
Lickham Bottom, near Hemyock, Devon
Mankinholes, near Todmorden, West Yorkshire
Minges, near Ware, Hertfordshire
Nasty, near Stevenage, Hertfordshire
Netherthong, near Huddersfield
Penistone, South Yorkshire
Piddlehinton, near Dorchester
Pisser Clough, near Widdop, West Yorkshire
Rimswell, East Riding of Yorkshire
Ring Burn, Glenwhilly, Dumfries, Scotland
Rotten Bottom, Tweeddale, Borders
Sandy Balls, near Fordingbridge, Hampshire
Shagg, near East Lulworth, Dorset
Shitlington Crags, near Wark, Northumberland
Shitterton, near Bere Regis, Dorset
Shitlington, (now Shillington) Bedfordshire
Slaggyford, near Haltwhistle, Northumberland
Spunkie, near Lugton, Ayrshire
Stublick Bog, near Haydon Bridge, Northumberland
The Bastard, near Campbelltown, Kintyre
Titty Ho, Raunds, Northamptonshire
Tongue of Gangsta, Orkney Islands
Turdees, near Chapelhall, North Lanarkshire
Twatt, Orkney
Wetwang, near Bridlington, Yorkshire

RIGHT UP YOUR STREET?
HOW DO YOU FANCY LIVING ON . . .

Ass House Lane, Harrow, Middlesex
Back Passage, City of London
Bogey Lane, Orpington, Bromley, Greater London
Butt Hole Road, Conisbrough, South Yorkshire
Carsick Hill Crescent, Sheffield
Catbrain Lane, Bristol
Clitterhouse Crescent, Barnet, North London
Crotch Crescent, Oxford
Dick Place, Edinburgh
Fanny Hands Lane, Market Rasen, Lincolnshire
Gravelly Bottom Road, nr Langley Heath, Kent
Grope Lane, Shrewsbury, Shropshire
Gropekunte Lane (now Opie Street), Norwich, Norfolk

Hardon Road, Wolverhampton
Hog's Turd Lane, Pirton, Hertfordshire
Letch Lane, Bourton-on-the-Water, Gloucestershire
Lickers Lane, Whiston, Prescot, Merseyside
Long Lover Lane, Halifax
Menlove Avenue, Liverpool
Minge Lane, Upton-upon-Severn, Worcestershire
Moisty Lane, Uttoxeter, Staffordshire
Nork Rise, Banstead, Surrey
Ogle Close, Merseyside
Old Sodom Lane, Dauntsey, Chippenham, Wiltshire
Pant-y-Felin Road, Swansea
Pennycomequick Hill, Plymouth, Devon
Pork Lane, Great Holland, near Frinton-on-Sea, Essex
Slag Lane, Haydock, St Helens Merseyside
Slutshole Lane, Besthorpe, Norfolk
Smellies Lane, Dundee
Spanker Lane, Nether Heage, Derbyshire
The Knob, Kings Sutton, Banbury
Tinkerbush Lane, Wantage, Oxfordshire
Tud Lane, Honingham, Norwich
Wham Bottom Lane, Healey, Lancashire
Whip-Ma-Whop-Ma-Gate, York
Winkle Street, Southampton

VISITING BRITAIN

In 2010, 29.627 million people visited Britain, spending an average of £563 per person and staying for seven days.

London remains the most popular destination for overseas visitors with more than 14.6 million spending time in the capital in 2010, where they spent over £8.6 billion.

The British Museum was Britain's most popular tourist attraction in 2010 during which it welcomed 5.8 million visitors, closely followed by Tate Modern (5.1 million), the National Gallery (5.0 million), the Natural History Museum (4.6 million) and the Science Museum (2.8 million).

Outside of London, Edinburgh Castle is the most popular tourist attraction drawing more than 1.2 million overseas visitors every year. Other top historic properties whose visitor numbers are counted in hundreds of thousands include: Stonehenge; the Old Royal Naval College, Greenwich; Hampton Court Palace; Chatsworth House; Leeds Castle and Blenheim Palace.

The seven most popular provincial visitor destinations are: Bath, Cambridge, the Cotswolds, the Lake District, Oxford, Stratford-upon-Avon and York.

According to the United Kingdom Tourism survey, UK residents took 119.4 million holiday trips and days out within the UK in 2010.

The 'stay-cation' – 57 million UK residents took short holidays in Great Britain of 1–3 nights in length accounting for a 63 per cent share while long holidays of 4 or more nights accounted for the remaining 37 per cent.

The most common age bracket of those UK residents who decided to holiday in Britain were those aged 55 and over.

A total of £20.8 billion was spent on domestic overnight tourism trips within the UK during 2010.

The Caravan Club was founded in 1907. Today it represents nearly 1 million members, operates around 200 main Caravan Club sites and 2,500 smaller certificated 'five-van' sites, known as CLs (Certificated Locations).

MOUNTAIN HIGH

Large quantities of ancient volcanic lava and ash known as the Borrowdale Volcanics covered the Lake District and this can still be seen in the form of mountains such as Helvellyn and Scafell Pike.

England's highest mountain is Scafell Pike in the Lake District measuring 3,209ft.

The highest mountain in Wales is Snowdon, which stands at 3,560ft.

The highest point in Great Britain is the summit of Ben Nevis in Scotland which soars skyward to 4,406ft.

WEATHER THE WEATHER

The highest temperature recorded in the UK was 38.5 °C (101.3 °F) at Brogdale, near Faversham, in the county of Kent, on 10 August 2003.

The lowest temperatures were recorded at –27.2 °C (–17.0 °F) at Braemar in the Grampian Mountains, Scotland, on 11 February 1895 and 10 January 1982 and Altnaharra, also in Scotland, on 30 December 1995.

BRITAIN'S LONGEST RIVERS

The longest river in the United Kingdom is the River Severn which flows through Wales and England, extending some 220 miles.

England: River Thames (215 miles)
Scotland: River Tay (117 miles)
N. Ireland: River Bann (76 miles)
Wales: River Tywi (64 miles)

BRITAIN'S DEEPEST CAVES

Ogof Ffynnon Ddu in Wales is 1,010ft deep and contains around 31 miles of passageways.
Peak Cavern in Speedwell Cavern, Derbyshire, in England is 814ft deep.
The deepest cave in Scotland is Cnoc nan Uamh ('hill of the caves') in Assynt at 272ft deep.

The deepest cave in Northern Ireland is Reyfad Pot in County Fermanagh, 633ft deep.

The longest cave system in the UK is the Easegill System in the Yorkshire Dales, with at least 45 miles of passageways.

HIGHEST SINGLE-DROP WATERFALLS

Eas a' Chual Aluinn (Scotland) 656ft
Steall Waterfall (Scotland) 393ft
Falls of Glomach (Scotland) 370ft
Devil's Appendix (Wales) 305ft
Pistyll y Llyn (Wales) 298ft
Cautley Spout (England) 249ft

BRITAIN'S LARGEST LAKES

N. Ireland: Lough Neagh (147.39 sq miles)
Scotland: Loch Lomond (27.46 sq miles)
England: Windermere (5.69 sq miles)
Wales: Llyn Tegid (Bala Lake) (1.87 sq miles)

DEEPEST LAKES

The United Kingdom's deepest lake is Loch Morar with a depth of 1,013ft at its deepest point. The second deepest is Loch Ness with a depth of at 748ft. The deepest lake in England is Wastwater with a depth of 258ft.

THE BROADS

The Norfolk Broads are not a natural phenomenon but are flooded medieval peat workings.

The Norfolk and Suffolk Broads are Britain's largest protected wetland and the third largest waterway with the status of a National Park.

The Norfolk Broads totals 188 miles, mostly in the county of Norfolk. Just over 125 miles of the Broads are navigable, covering a total of seven rivers and sixty-three Broads.

2

BATTLES & WARS

BATTLES IN BRITAIN

A small selection of engagements famous and not so famous fought on British soil.

10 August 991 The Battle of Maldon. Anglo-Saxon troops, led by Byrhtnoth, Ealdorman of Essex, were defeated by a band of Viking raiders near Maldon in Essex.

18 October 1016 The Battle of Assandune. Fought between the armies of Canute the Dane and Edmund Ironside in Essex, arguably near the village now known as Ashingdon. Folklore tells that a halt was called to the bloody battle and Ironside issued a challenge of single combat with Canute to settle the matter. Canute declared that they should divide the kingdom instead, Canute taking all that lay north of Watling Street, Ironside could have all to the south of it. This was agreed but Canute was to become the overall King of England after Ironside died less than two months later. Many suggest Ironside was killed at the behest of Canute.

14 October 1066 The Battle of Hastings was actually fought on Senlac Hill, at what is now known as Battle near Hastings, East Sussex. It was the decisive victory for the invading Norman army of William the Bastard over King Harold Godwinson of England. Battle Abbey was founded by the new King William 'The Conqueror' where the battle was fought as a memorial to the dead, as an act of atonement for the bloodshed and as a very public symbol of the Norman triumph.

22 August 1138 The Battle of the Standard, also known as The Battle of Northallerton, was fought on Cowton Moor near Northallerton, Yorkshire. Scottish forces led by King David I of Scotland were defeated by an English army commanded by William of Aumale.

4 August 1265 The Battle of Evesham, Worcestershire. Royalist forces led by Prince Edward (later Edward I) defeated the forces of the rebel barons led by Simon de Montfort and Peter de Montfort, who both lost their lives in this battle.

27 April 1296 The Battle of Dunbar. A decisive victory for the English led by John de Warenne, 6th Earl of Surrey over the Scots led by John Balliol.

11 September 1297 The Battle of Stirling Bridge. An English force led by John de Warenne was defeated by a far smaller Scottish force led by William Wallace and Andrew de Moray.

22 July 1298 The Battle of Falkirk. On his return from a campaign in France, Edward I organised an army, including a huge number of Welsh longbowmen, that he would lead personally against the Scots. He met the forces led by William Wallace at Falkirk and achieved a decisive victory over them.

24 June 1314 The Battle of Bannockburn a victory for the Scots led by Robert the Bruce over an English force led by Edward II.

23 September 1459 The Battle of Blore Heath, fought neat Market Drayton, Shropshire. A surprise attack by Lord Audley failed, he lost his life and the Yorkists gained a victory.

12 October 1459 The Battle of Ludford Bridge, Shropshire. A victory for the Lancastrian forces led by Richard, Duke of York.

10 July 1460 The Battle of Northampton, a significant victory for the Yorkists led by the Earl of Warwick.

2 February 1461 The Battle of Mortimer's Cross, fought near Wigmore, Herefordshire, was a decisive victory for the Yorkists during the Wars of the Roses.

29 March 1461 The Battle of Towton, Yorkshire, described by some historians as 'the largest and bloodiest battle ever fought on English soil', saw Edward of York defeat the belligerents of the House of Lancaster to become King Edward IV of England.

25 April 1464 The Battle of Hedgeley Moor fought to the north of the village of Glanton in Northumberland. A Lancastrian army led by the Duke of Somerset was defeated by a Yorkist army led by John Neville, 1st Marquess of Montagu.

15 May 1464 The Battle of Hexham in Northumberland. John Neville, leading a modest force of 3,000–4,000 men, routed the Lancastrian force capturing a number of rebel leaders who would later be executed.

26 July 1469 The Battle of Edgecote Moor, Banbury, Oxfordshire. The Earl of Warwick leading a rebel Lancastrian army achieved victory over the Yorkist force led by the Earl of Pembroke.

20 March 1469 The Battle of Nibley Green, Gloucestershire. The last battle fought in England entirely between the private armies of feudal magnates, namely Thomas Talbot, 2nd Viscount Lisle and those of William Berkeley, 2nd Baron Berkeley. The forces of Baron Berkeley were victorious.

4 May 1471 The Battle of Tewkesbury in Gloucestershire was a decisive victory for the Yorkist forces led by Edward IV and Richard of Gloucester.

22 August 1485 The Battle of Bosworth Field saw a decisive Lancastrian victory, the death of Richard III, the end of the House of Plantagenet, the end of the Wars of the Roses and the ascent of the House of Tudor to the throne.

17 June 1497 The Battle of Deptford Bridge. Cornish rebels led by Michael An Gof were defeated by troops led by King Henry VII.

9 September 1513 The Battle of Flodden, near Branxton, Northumberland. An invading Scots army under James IV was defeated by an English army in a cruel and bloody battle during which King James himself was killed in combat.

24 November 1542 The Battle of Solway Moss. A Scottish army under Lord Robert Maxwell was beaten by an English army led by Sir Thomas Wharton.

28 August 1640 The Battle of Newburn, Northumberland. A Scottish Covenanter army led by General Alexander Leslie defeated an English army under Edward, Lord Conway.

23 September 1642 The Battle of Powick Bridge, Worcester. The first major cavalry engagement of the English Civil War and a victory for the Royalists.

23 October 1642 The Battle of Edgehill, Warwickshire, the first pitched battle of the English Civil War.

19 January 1643 The Battle of Braddock Down, Cornwall. A victory for Royalist forces under Sir Ralph Hopton that secured Cornwall for King Charles.

30 June 1643 The Battle of Adwalton Moor, West Yorkshire. Vastly superior numbers of Royalist troops led by the Earl of Newcastle defeated a far smaller Parliamentarian force led by Sir Thomas Fairfax.

13 July 1643 The Battle of Roundway Down, near Devizes, Wiltshire. A Royalist cavalry force under Lord Wilmot won a crushing victory over the Parliamentarians under Sir William Waller.

11 October 1643 The Battle of Winceby, Lincolnshire, resulted in a decisive victory for Parliamentary forces led by the Earl of Manchester and Oliver Cromwell.

2 July1644 The Battle of Marston Moor, Yorkshire. The combined forces of the Scottish Covenanters under the Earl of Leven and the English Parliamentarians under Lord Fairfax and the Earl of Manchester defeated the Royalists commanded by Prince Rupert and the Marquess of Newcastle.

14 June 1645 The Battle of Naseby. The main army of King Charles I led by the king and Prince Rupert of the Rhine was destroyed by the Parliamentarian New Model Army commanded by Sir Thomas Fairfax and Oliver Cromwell.

6 July 1685 The Battle of Sedgemoor. The final Battle of The Monmouth Rebellion. The Royal army of James II defeated the rebel army of James Scott, 1st Duke of Monmouth. The defeated duke escaped from the battlefield but was arrested in Dorset and he was executed at Tower Hill on 15 July 1685.

21 August 1689 The Battle of Dunkeld, part of the first Jacobite rising, was fought in the streets around Dunkeld Cathedral. Jacobite clans supporting the deposed King James VII of Scotland were defeated by a Scottish government regiment of covenanters who supported William of Orange, King of Scotland.

21 September 1745 The Battle of Prestonpans. A Hanoverian army under the command of Sir John Cope was defeated – in ten minutes – by Jacobite forces under the command of Prince Charles Edward Stuart and Lord George Murray.

16 April 1746 The Battle of Culloden. The Jacobite army led by Charles Stuart ('Bonnie Prince Charlie') suffered a crushing defeat at the hands of an English force led by the Duke of Cumberland and brought the Jacobite Rebellion to an end. This was the last major action to be fought on British soil between British citizens.

25 February 1797 Irish-American Colonel William Tate and his force of 1,000–1,500 soldiers of *La Legion Noire* surrendered after The Battle of Fishguard – the last attempted invasion of Great Britain.

TWENTY-FIVE FACTS ABOUT BRITISH CASTLES

The Nine Castles of Knuckle are a group of ancient castles found in the extinct area of Knuckle, which would today be located on the very far corner of the north-east coast of Aberdeenshire in the Buchan area of Scotland.

Caerphilly Castle is the largest castle in Wales and the second largest in Great Britain.

The keep at Bridgnorth Castle in Shropshire, reduced to a ruin by Parliamentary forces in 1624 during the English Civil War, now leans at an angle of 17 degrees – three times further than the Leaning Tower of Pisa.

The first use of cannon to attack a castle in Scotland was in 1334 when Regent Andrew Moray attacked Dundarg Castle.

One of the longest sieges of any British castle occurred when Parliamentarian forces laid siege to Donnington Castle in Berkshire from October 1644 until April 1646.

Dover Castle, constructed in the form recognisable today during the reign of Henry II, was such an important defensive bastion it became known as the 'Key to England'.

Ravenscraig Castle, built in 1460 by order of King James II, is believed to be the first to be built to withstand cannon fire and provide for artillery defence in Scotland.

Cubbie Roo's Castle, built in 1145 on Wyre, Orkney, was one of the earliest stone castles to be built in Scotland.

New Buckenham Castle keep in Norfolk has the largest in diameter to be found in England.

Windsor Castle in Berkshire is the largest inhabited castle in the world.

Haughley Castle, near Bury St Edmunds in Suffolk, is one of the largest mottes in Britain at 80ft wide and 80ft high.

Rochester Castle keep is the tallest Norman keep in Britain – it rises to 115ft.

Someries Castle in Bedfordshire dates from the fifteenth century and is believed to be one of the first brick buildings in England.

Chepstow Castle in Monmouthshire, begun in 1068, is the oldest surviving post-Roman stone fortification in Britain.

Deal Castle in Kent is one of the most impressive of the Device Forts or Henrician Castles built by Henry VIII between 1539 and 1540. It is shaped like a Tudor rose.

Caerphilly Castle is one of the greatest surviving fortresses of the medieval western world.

The thirteenth-century Loch Doon Castle once sat on an island in the middle of Loch Doon in Scotland. During the 1930s, the level of the loch was raised in connection with the Galloway hydro-electric scheme. The island became submerged but the outer shell of the castle was dismantled and re-erected in about 1935 on the shore near Craigmulloch Farm, where it may still be seen today.

Thornbury Castle, begun by Edward Stafford, Duke of Buckingham in 1511, was the last major fortified manor house to be built in England.

Castell Dinas, a hillfort and castle in southern Powys, really does stand high on a hill at 1,476ft (SO179301) up – it is the highest castle to be found in England and Wales.

Kenilworth Castle, Warwickshire, is one of the largest ruined castles in England.

Penhow Castle, built by Sir William St Maur in the early thirteenth century, is the oldest inhabited castle in Wales.

The last castle in Britain to be besieged was Blair Castle, in 1746, when Lord George Murray laid siege to it during the Jacobite uprising.

Exeter Castle, built by William the Conqueror in 1068, has one of the earliest surviving stone gatehouses in England.

Beaumaris Castle in Wales, begun in 1295, is the most technically perfect medieval castle in Britain.

The siege of Kenilworth Castle in 1266 was broken after six months when the defenders were forced to surrender due to an outbreak of dysentery.

SOLDIERS OF THE QUEEN – SOME FACTS ABOUT THE BRITISH ARMY DURING THE REIGN OF QUEEN VICTORIA

Khaki was known to be worn by some regiments from as early as the Indian Mutiny in 1858 but was only formally introduced for wear by British units in India in 1878.

For the majority of the nineteenth century the officers and men of the British Army retained scarlet tunics as their day-to-day working uniform and was only superseded by the introduction of the khaki Service Dress jacket and trousers in 1902.

The Glengarry cap, initially introduced as the undress cap for Scottish Regiments in 1852, was adopted by the majority of English Line Infantry regiments in plain blue in the 1870s and remained the standard headgear for other ranks up to the 1890s.

The 'blue cloth' Home Service helmets for parades, so indicative of Victorian soldiers, were introduced in 1878.

Queen Victoria's soldiers were granted a pay rise for private soldiers from 8*d* to a whopping 1*s* a day!

The most common destination for Queen Victoria's soldiers sent on foreign service was India. To give some indication of the number of campaigns and military expeditions carried out during Her Majesty's reign, the India General Service Medal, instituted in 1854 and awarded until 1895, had a total of 24 clasps sanctioned.

The Crimean War of the 1850s was fought between the Russian Empire and an alliance of the French, British and Ottoman Empires and the Kingdom of Sardinia. The war included such notable actions as the Siege of Sebastopol, the Battles of the Alma, Inkerman and Balaclava where the Charge of the Light Brigade took place on 25 October 1854.

The Battle of Balaclava is also remembered for the staunch bravery of the 93rd Highlanders who, standing just two ranks deep, withstood repeated attacks by a Russian force of vastly superior numbers. *The Times* correspondent, William H. Russell, wrote that he could see nothing between the charging Russians and the British regiment's base of operations at Balaclava but the 'thin red streak tipped with a line of steel' of the 93rd. This stand led the 93rd Highlanders to be remembered in history as the 'Thin Red Line' and a legendary symbol of British sangfroid in battle.

The Indian Rebellion of 1857 began as a mutiny of Sepoys of the British East India Company's army, in the town of Meerut on 10 May 1857.

The Cardwell Reforms, the greatest reforms in the British Army during the nineteenth century, were enacted over the years 1868–74.

The Battle of Rorke's Drift, when a garrison of just over 150 British and colonial troops, many of them members of the 2nd Battalion, 24th Foot (The Warwickshire Regiment), successfully defended the outpost against an intense assault by 3,000–4,000 Zulu warriors, was fought on 22–23 January 1879 during the Anglo-Zulu War. Eleven Victoria Crosses were awarded to the defenders of Rorke's Drift, seven of them to soldiers of the 2nd/24th Foot – the greatest number of the award ever received in a single action by one regiment. The 2nd Battalion, 24th Foot did contain many recruits from Wales at the time of Rorke's Drift but only became the South Wales Borderers in 1881.

In 1881 the Childers Reforms abolished the old British Army numbered regiment system in favour of named county regiments.

The Battle of Omdurman, fought on 2 September 1898 during the Sudan War, saw the last great cavalry charge of the British Army.

The last major war fought by Queen Victoria's soldiers was the Second Anglo-Boer War against the Afrikaans-speaking Dutch settlers of two independent Boer republics, the South African Republic (Transvaal Republic) and the Orange Free State in South Africa, from 11 October 1899 to 31 May 1902.

SOME FACTS ABOUT THE VICTORIA CROSS

The Victoria Cross (VC) is the highest military decoration awarded for valour 'in the face of the enemy' to members of the British and Commonwealth armed forces and to civilians under military command regardless of rank or arm of service.

The Victoria Cross has precedence over all other orders, decorations and medals.

The Victoria Cross came into existence when Queen Victoria signed the Royal Warrant instigating the award on 29 January 1856 and approved a specimen Victoria Cross medal itself on 3 March of the same year.

It was originally intended that Victoria Crosses would be cast from the bronze cascabels of two cannon that were captured from the Russians at the Siege of Sebastopol during the Crimean War.

Only one company of jewellers, Hancocks of London, has been responsible for the production of every Victoria Cross awarded since its inception.

The names of the first 85 servicemen to be awarded the VC were published in the *London Gazette* of 24 February 1857.

The first investitures of the VC took place at Hyde Park on 26 June 1857 where Queen Victoria personally decorated 62 recipients.

The original (1856) specification for the Victoria Cross stipulated that the ribbon should be 'red' for army recipients and 'blue' for naval recipients. The dark blue ribbon was abolished soon after the formation of the Royal Air Force on 1 April 1918. On 22 May 1920 King George V signed a warrant which stated that all recipients would now receive a red ribbon and the living recipients of the naval version were required to exchange their ribbons to the new colour.

In the case of an act of gallantry being performed by a squadron, ship's company or a detached body of men in which all are deemed equally brave and deserving of the Victoria Cross, a ballot is drawn. The officers select one officer, the NCOs select one individual and the private soldiers or seamen select two individuals. In all, 46 awards of the Victoria Cross have been awarded by ballot.

The greatest number of Victoria Crosses won on a single day is eighteen, at the Second Relief of Lucknow on 16 November 1857 during the Indian Mutiny.

The greatest number of Victoria Crosses won in a single action is twenty-eight, for actions throughout the Second Relief of Lucknow, 14–22 November 1857.

The greatest number of Victoria Crosses won by a single unit during a single action is eleven, to the 2nd/24th Foot, for the defence of Rorke's Drift, 22–23 January 1879, during the Zulu War.

Only three people have been awarded a bar to denote a second award of the Victoria Cross, namely: Captain Noel Chavasse and Lieutenant-Colonel Arthur Martin-Leake, both doctors in the Royal Army Medical Corps who received their VCs for rescuing wounded under fire, and New Zealander Charles Upham, an infantryman, for combat actions in Crete and the Western Desert during the Second World War.

Since its inception there have been 1,356 awards of the Victoria Cross.

The most recent recipient of the Victoria Cross is Lance Corporal Johnson Gideon Beharry, 1st Battalion, Princess of Wales's Royal Regiment for twice saving members of his unit from ambushes on 1 May and again on 11 June 2004 at Al-Amarah, Iraq. Beharry was formally invested with the Victoria Cross by Queen Elizabeth II on 27 April 2005.

SOME INTERESTING FACTS ABOUT THE FIRST WORLD WAR

Great Britain declared war with Germany at 11.00 p.m. on 4 August 1914.

When war was declared, the British Regular Army comprised four regiments of Foot Guards, 69 infantry regiments, three Household and 25 other cavalry regiments of the line, plus corps troops such as the Artillery, the Engineers and the Medical Corps. The British Army had 125,000 professional officers, non-commissioned officers (NCOs) and soldiers.

Kitchener's famous call to arms, 'Your King and Country Need You', was first published on 11 August 1914. The soldiers who joined under this scheme became known as 'Kitchener Men'.

The main units of the British Expeditionary Force totalling 80,000 troops landed in France on 12 August 1914.

By 21 August 1914 Kitchener had his first 100,000 recruits and what became known as 'K1', the first six divisions of the 'New Army', were approved by the War Office. There were to be five 'New' armies formed under the Kitchener scheme, meaning that most infantry regiments received three New Army battalions, while some, such as the Middlesex and the Manchester regiments, had many more.

In September 1914 an average 33,000 recruits were enlisting nationally on a daily basis to serve in Britain's armed forces.

The first engagement between the British and German forces on the Western Front during the First World War occurred on 23 August 1914 in what proved to be the first day of the Battle of Mons.

The first offensive bombing raid by a Zeppelin on Great Britain took place along the Norfolk coast on 19 January 1915.

On 25 April 1915 landings were made by British, Australian and New Zealand troops at Anzac Cove and Cape Helles on the Gallipoli Peninsula.

Britain had an all-volunteer army until 2 March 1916 when the Military Service Act (1916), the first statute of full conscription in British military history, came into force.

Lieutenant William Leefe Robinson of 39 Squadron, flying his B.E.2c night fighter, on the night of 2/3 September 1916, was the first British pilot to shoot down a German zeppelin (L.21) over Britain during the First World War. Robinson was awarded the Victoria Cross and continued to serve with distinction at home and in action over the Western Front. Tragically, having survived the war, he lost his life during the Spanish 'flu pandemic of 1918.

The Battle of Jutland fought in the North Sea off Denmark from 31 May–1 June 1916, was one of the few major engagements between British and German Navies fought during the First World War. Both sides retired from the battle, each declaring a victory.

1 July 1916 was the first day of the Battle of the Somme on the Western Front. On this single day the British Army suffered almost 60,000 casualties.

Broadly speaking, during a year on the Western Front, a British Tommy might expect to spend about 70 days on the front line, with another 30 in nearby support trenches. A further 120 days might be spent in reserve and 70 days might be spent at rest. The amount of leave varied, with perhaps a total of two weeks being granted during the year.

Tanks were first used in combat by the British Army at Flers-Courcelette, during the Battle of the Somme on 15 September 1916. When the new British secret weapon was first despatched to the front line, their secret was maintained by any reference in their shipment being referred to as 'tanks', as in *water* tanks, and the name stuck.

The war spread into new theatres including Egypt, Mesopotamia and Palestine. One of the most bloody battles, the Second Battle of Gaza, took place in Southern Palestine on 17 April 1917. Almost 6,000 British, Anzac and Imperial troops were killed or wounded on this one day of battle.

The new offensive on the Western Front in 1917 was fought between 31 July and 6 November 1917. They called it the Battle of Passchendaele. The casualty figures for this action are disputed but the combined casualties for the allied forces of Britain, Canada, Australia and France are conservatively estimated to have numbered 200,000; other estimates state a figure of more than double.

The Royal Air Force was formed by the amalgamation of the Royal Flying Corps and the Royal Naval Air Service on 1 April 1918.

The closing battles of the First World War on the Western Front became known as the 'Hundred Days' Offensive' by the Allies and were fought along the Hindenburg Line between 8 August and 11 November 1918.

The Armistice was declared at 11.00 a.m. on 11 November 1918.

Britain celebrated Peace Day after the Treaty of Versailles had been signed. The bulk of the surviving servicemen and women had returned home to a grand Victory March through London, and services of thanksgiving, public events and dinners were held across the country on 19 July 1919.

According to figures produced in the 1920s by the Central Statistical Office, the total British armed forces casualties killed in action, died of wounds, disease or injury or missing presumed dead during the First World War numbered 956,703. Of these some 526,816 have no known grave and are commemorated on memorials to the missing such as Thiepval (Northern France) and the Menin Gate (Belgium).

The first British Legion Poppy Day was held on Friday 11 November 1921 and raised £106,000 for returned servicemen in need or the dependants of those who had fallen in the First World War.

SOME INTERESTING FACTS ABOUT THE SECOND WORLD WAR

At 11.15 a.m. on 3 September 1939, Prime Minister Neville Chamberlain addressed the British nation by radio and announced 'this country is at war with Germany.'

Conscription of men aged 18 to 41 was introduced in Britain from the outbreak of war on 3 September 1939 under the National Service (Armed Forces) Act 1939.

The 2nd Battalion, The Royal Norfolk Regiment was the first complete infantry unit of the British Expeditionary Force to land in France in 1939. It was also members of the 2nd Battalion, The Royal Norfolk Regiment who were awarded the first army decorations during the Second World War when Captain Peter Barclay and Cpl M.H. 'Mick' Davis were respectively granted the Military Cross and Military Medal for their gallantry during a scouting mission and subsequent contact with the enemy on the night of 3/4 January 1940.

Winston Churchill became wartime coalition Prime Minister on 10 May 1940.

The first appeal for volunteers to join the Local Defence Volunteers (later retitled the Home Guard) was made by Anthony Eden in a radio broadcast between the 9 o'clock news and a documentary entitled *The Voice of the Nazi* on 14 May 1940. Thousands offered their services immediately and over the course of the war over 1.5 million men served in what affectionately became known as 'Dad's Army'.

During the period of 26 May and the early hours of 3 June 1940, tens of thousands of British, French and Belgian troops were evacuated from the beaches and harbour of Dunkirk, France, in what was known as Operation Dynamo. This remarkable achievement was soon dubbed 'The Miracle of Dunkirk'.

The first attack on England's mainland during the Second World War is officially recorded as taking place at 4.00 a.m. on 10 May 1940 when twenty-three incendiary bombs fell on East Stour Farm at Chilham, near Canterbury in Kent.

Churchill's famous speech in which he stated: 'Never in the field of human conflict was so much owed by so many to so few', made on 20 August 1940, was a tribute to the ongoing efforts of the Royal Air Force pilots fighting the Battle of Britain.

ARP Warden Thomas Hopper Alderson was the first person to be directly awarded the George Cross (published in the supplement to the *London Gazette* of 27 September 1940, dated 30 September 1940) for his gallant rescues of trapped civilians during air raids in Bridlington, Yorkshire, during August 1940.

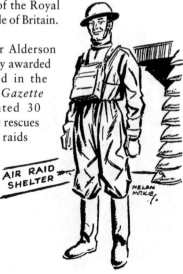

AIR RAID SHELTER

The first major day of the blitz offensive on London was 7 September 1940. At 4.35 p.m. the first bombs fell on Ford's motor works at Dagenham, followed by a massive drop of both HE (high explosive) and incendiary bombs upon Beckton Gas Works, at the time the largest in Europe. Then followed the bombing of the London Docks, factories, warehouses and rows of terraced houses and tenements in the East End. London was then bombed consecutively during the day or night for the next 57 days.

The Luftwaffe blitz on London destroyed or damaged more than a million houses and more than 20,000 civilians were killed but London carried on and the spirit of the people of London remained unbroken.

The Battle of Taranto in Italy on 11–12 November 1940 was the first all-aircraft ship-to-ship naval attack in history. It resulted in the destruction of one battleship, with two further damaged and a decisive British victory won by the Swordfish aircraft from 813, 815, 819 and 824 Naval Air Squadrons.

The British nation was shocked by the sinking of HMS *Hood* by the German battleship *Bismarck* during the Battle of the Denmark Strait on 24 May 1941. Out of a crew of the 1,418, only three men survived the sinking, namely: Ordinary Signalman Ted Briggs, Able Seaman Robert Tilburn and Midshipman William John Dundas.

On 15 February 1942 a deputation made their way under the British flag to discuss terms at the Ford Motor Factory, Singapore, led by Lieutenant-General Arthur Percival who formally surrendered shortly after 17.15 hours and an agreement was made all hostilities were to cease at 20.30 hours. The majority of the soldiers on the island spent the rest of the war in a living hell as prisoners in the hands of the Japanese. Despite all the horrors they faced they never forgot they were soldiers.

On Thursday 18 December 1941 the National Service (No. 2) Act was passed by Parliament and the first Royal Proclamation calling up women under the National Service Acts was signed by the king.

The Second Battle of El Alamein was fought in the Western Desert from 23 October to 4 November 1942. It was a decisive victory for the Allied forces led by 8th Army 'Desert Rat' commander Lieutenant-General Bernard Montgomery and turned the tide of the entire North African campaign.

Blue Cock 'Royal Blue', bred by and trained at HM King George VI's Pigeon Loft, Sandringham, and operating out of Bircham Newton, was the first pigeon to bring a message from a force-landed aircrew on the Continent during the Second World War. Released by the crew in Holland on 10 October 1940 at 07.20 hours, the young bird arrived with its message at Sandringham at 11.30 hours the same day. This efficient pigeon was recognised for this action by the award of the Dickin Medal, 'the animals' VC', in March 1945.

HITLER WILL SEND
NO
WARNING

PRACTISE PUTTING ON YOUR GAS MASK

1. Hold your breath. (*To breathe in gas may be fatal.*) **2.** Hold mask in front of face, thumbs inside straps. **3.** Thrust chin well forward into mask. Pull straps as far over head as they will go. **4.** Run finger round face-piece taking care head-straps are not twisted.

MAKE SURE IT FITS

See that the rubber fits snugly at sides of jaw and under chin. The head-straps should be adjusted to hold the mask firmly. To test for fit, hold a piece of paper to end of mask and breathe in. The paper should stick.

Arrows indicate points needing particular attention

On 16 May 1943 bombers of 617 Squadron RAF flew out from Scampton in Lincolnshire in Operation Chastise to attack the Möhne, Eder and Sorpe Dams of the Ruhr Valley with the specially designed 'bouncing bombs' invented by Barnes Wallis and entered history as 'the Dam Busters.'

6 June 1944, D-Day – British and Allied forces achieve a successful landing on the beaches of Normandy to begin the liberation of North-Western Europe from the forces of the Third Reich.

The Battle of Kohima in Nagaland, British India, was fought from April 1944 until the final hard-won victory for the Allies on 22 June 1944 at the cost of over 4,000 lives. The bravery and sacrifice of the men of the 'Forgotten Army' throughout the campaign in India and Burma should never be overlooked.

In Operation Catechism, the German battleship *Tirpitz* was struck by a force of 32 Lancasters from Nos 9 and 617 Squadrons of the Royal Air Force on 12 November 1944.

On 8 May 1945 VE (Victory in Europe) Day was celebrated across Britain to mark the unconditional surrender of the German armed forces and the end of Hitler's Third Reich.

VJ (Victory in Japan) Day was celebrated in Britain on 15 August 1945 to mark the unconditional surrender of Japan and the end of the Second World War.

An estimated 383,800 United Kingdom service personnel and 67,100 civilians died in the Second World War.

THE BAEDEKER BLITZ

After the failure of the German bombing campaigns to destroy airfields and London in 1940/1, Hitler planned to break British morale by attempting to destroy the picturesque and historic cities of England. Spurred on by the RAF bombing raids on the historic German cities of Lübeck and Rostock in early 1942, the British cities chosen for the reprisal raids were selected from the German *Baedeker* tourist guide to Britain. German propagandist Baron Gustav Braun von Sturm is reported to have said after the first attack of the campaign 'We shall go out and bomb every building in Britain marked with three stars in the

Baedeker Guide' and thus the so called 'Three-Star Blitz' or 'Baedeker Blitz' became the name given by the British to these infamous raids on Exeter, Bath, Norwich, York and Canterbury between April and June 1942.

THE BOYS *AND GIRL* OF THE OLD BRIGADE

Wiltshire man William Hiseland (1620–1732/3) was the last survivor of the English Civil War. Fighting on the side of the Royalists, Hiseland was present at the Battle of Edgehill (23 October 1642). He retired with rank of sergeant after an incredible eighty years of service to the king and became one of the first old soldiers to be admitted to the Royal Hospital, Chelsea. The inscription on Hiseland's tomb in the Royal Hospital's burial ground reads as follows:

> Here Lies WILLIAM HISELAND
> A Vetran if ever Soldier was
> Who merited well a Pension
> If Long Service be a Merit
> Having served upwards of the Days of Man
> Antient but not Superannuated
> Engaged in a series of Wars Civil as well as Foreign
> Yet not maimed or worn out by either
> His Complexion was fresh & florid
> His Health hale & hearty
> His Memory exact & ready
> In Stature He exceeded the Military size
> In Strength He surpassed the prime of Youth
> and What rendered his Age Still more Patriarchal
> When above one Hundred Years Old
> He took unto him a Wife
> Read Fellow Soldiers and Reflect
> That there is a Spiritual Warfare
> As well as a Warfare Temporal
> Born vj of August 1620 Died vij of Feb. 1732 Aged 112

Joseph Sutherland RN (1789–1890) was the last English survivor of the Battle of Trafalgar (1805).

Private Morris Shea (1795–1892), a veteran of the 2nd Battalion, 73rd Regiment of Foot, was the last living British veteran of the Napoleonic Wars.

Lieutenant-Colonel Frank Bourne OBE DCM (1854–1945) was the last known survivor of the Battle of Rorke's Drift, 22–23 January 1879, during the Zulu War. At the time of the action Bourne was the Colour Sergeant of 2/24th Foot and was awarded the DCM for 'outstanding coolness and courage' during the battle. In the 1964 film *Zulu*, Bourne was played by Nigel Green. Green was considerably older (about 40 years old) and taller than Bourne, who was aged 24 and stood 5ft 6in at the time of the battle.

The last survivor of the Boer War (1899–1902) was George Frederick Ives who had served in the Imperial Yeomanry. Born in Brighton on 12 November 1881, he emigrated and spent his later life in Canada where he died on 12 April 1993 aged 111 years and 146 days.

The last British fighting Tommy to fight in the trenches of the Western Front (he was present at the Battle of Passchendaele) was Henry John 'Harry' Patch who served as a private (army number 29295) with 7th Battalion, the Duke of Cornwall's Light Infantry. He died on 25 July 2009 aged 111 years and 38 days.

The last member of the Royal Naval Air Service, last survivor of the Battle of Jutland and last surviving airman serving at the time of the creation of the Royal Air Force in 1918 was Henry William Allingham who died on 18 July 2009 aged 113 years and 42 days.

The last person to see combat in the First World War was Claude Choules, a career serviceman of the Royal Navy. He was also the last veteran to have served in both world wars, the last surviving seaman from the First World War and the last military witness to the scuttling of the German fleet in Scapa Flow. Born in Pershore, Worcestershire, on 3 March 1901, after serving in the First World War Choules was sent to Australia on loan as a the Royal Navy instructor in 1926. He met his future wife on the voyage and they decided to make it their new home. Claude Choules passed away on at Perth in Western Australia on 5 May 2011 aged 110 years and 63 days. He was given a naval funeral in Fremantle.

Florence Beatrice Green was the last living person to have served in the British forces during the First World War; indeed she was the last surviving veteran of the First World War. Born at Edmonton in London on 19 February 1901, she joined the Women's Royal Air Force in September 1918 where she served as an officers' mess steward on the airfields at Narborough and Marham in Norfolk. Florence moved to King's Lynn in 1920 where she lived until her death on 4 February 2012 aged 100 years and 350 days.

3

ROYALTY

TEN CURIOUS FACTS
ABOUT BRITISH MONARCHS

King Henry I died on 1 December 1135 after eating 'a surfeit of lampreys' (an eel-like fish) of which he was rather fond while he was in Normandy. His body was sewn into the hide of a bull to preserve him for his return journey to England and he was buried at Reading Abbey.

According to a story recorded by Thomas de la Moore, King Edward II was assassinated at Berkley Castle on 11 October 1327 by a red-hot poker being thrust up his anus.

George Plantagenet, 1st Duke of Clarence, was 'privately executed' at the Tower of London on 18 February 1478 on the orders of his brother, King Edward IV. Tradition has it he was a heavy drinker and was suitable despatched by being drowned in a butt of Malmsey wine.

Elizabeth I (1533–1603) was the first British monarch to have a fully fitted flushing toilet.

Lady Jane Grey was queen for a mere nine days from 10 July 1553 until she was removed and later beheaded by Mary Tudor. What is little known is that at the time she was only sixteen years old.

King Charles II (1630–85) had numerous mistresses and had fourteen known illegitimate children.

The tradition of standing during the '*Hallelujah' chorus* began on 23 March 1743 when King George II was attending the performance and when it began the king rose to his feet. It is unclear why he stood up; he could well have been stretching his legs, as he was known to do. It is also possible that dear King George, who was partially deaf, mistook the opening notes for the national anthem.

King George III struggled with mental illness in later life and having become 'permanently insane' in 1811, he lived out the rest of his life in seclusion at Windsor Castle where he died in 1820.

After the death of her beloved husband Prince Albert in 1861, Queen Victoria ordered the staff at the retreat they loved, Osborne House on the Isle of Wight, to continue to deliver the hot water for his shave to his room.

Queen Elizabeth II loves corgis. She has owned more than thirty during her reign, starting with Susan who was given to her as a present when she was but a princess back in 1944.

THE SIX WIVES OF HENRY VIII – A RHYME TO REMEMBER THEIR FATES

'Divorced, beheaded, died; Divorced beheaded survived'

Catherine of Aragon (1485–1536): Divorced
Anne Boleyn (1501–36): Beheaded kneeling upright by sword
Jane Seymour (1508–37): Died of postnatal complications
Anne of Cleves (1515–57): Divorced, or rather, annulled
Catherine Howard (b. between 1518 and
    1524–42): Beheaded by axe, head on
    block
Katherine Parr (1512–48): Survived and
    outlived Henry VIII

A FAR FROM LOYAL TOAST

Jacobite supporters and sympathisers (those dedicated to the restoration of the House of Stuart to the thrones of England and Scotland) drank a toast to 'The little gentleman in the black velvet waistcoat' – a reference to the mole that raised a molehill against which William III's horse stumbled and unseated its rider. The king died from complications caused by his injuries.

THE ROYAL RESIDENCES OF HM THE QUEEN

Buckingham Palace (London)
Windsor Castle (Berkshire)
Palace of Holyrood (Edinburgh)
Sandringham (Norfolk)
Balmoral Castle (Aberdeenshire)
Craigowan Lodge (Aberdeenshire)
Delnadamph Lodge (Aberdeenshire)

SOME FORMER PALACES AND RESIDENCES OF BRITISH ROYALTY

Palace of Beaulieu, Chelmsford, Essex (Henry VIII, Edward VI and Elizabeth I)

Beaumont Palace, Oxford (Henry I – Edward II)

Bridewell Palace, London (Henry VIII – Edward VI)

Cadzow Castle, South Lanarkshire (residence of Scottish monarchs David I, Alexander II, Alexander III, John, Robert I and Mary, Queen of Scots)

Caernarfon Castle (Edward I)

Dunfermline Palace, Fife (seat of the successive Kings of Scots 1500–1650)

Edinburgh Castle (residence of the successive Kings of Scots from the eleventh to the seventeenth centuries)

Eltham Palace, Kent (Edward II – Henry VIII)

Hampton Court Palace, London (owned by the Crown since Henry VIII)

King's Langley Palace, Hertfordshire (Plantagenets to the Tudor monarchs 1276–1558)

Nonsuch Palace, Surrey (Henry VIII)

Oatlands Palace, Weybridge, Surrey (Henry VIII, Elizabeth I and the Stuart line)

Royal Pavilion Brighton, East Sussex (George IV – Queen Victoria)

Theobald's Palace, Hertfordshire (James I and Charles I)

QUEEN VICTORIA'S CHILDREN

Queen Victoria and Prince Albert had nine children:

Victoria Adelaide Mary Louisa, the Princess Royal (1840–1901). She married the German Emperor Frederick II and became the German Empress. Her eldest son became Kaiser Wilhelm II 'Kaiser Bill' of Germany, who led Germany, our enemy during the First World War.

Albert Edward known as 'Bertie' (1841–1910). Became Edward VII; one of his sons became George V, the monarch who led Britain and the British Empire during the First World War.

Princess Alice Maud Mary, Grand Duchess of Hesse (1843–78). Married Louis IV, Grand Duke of Hesse. One of her daughters became Empress Alexandra Feodorovna (the wife of Emperor Nicholas II of Russia) and the maternal great-grandmother of Prince Philip, Duke of Edinburgh, consort of Queen Elizabeth II.

Alfred Ernest Albert, Duke of Saxe-Coburg and Gotha (1844–1900). Married Grand Duchess Maria Alexandrovna of Russia.

Princess Helena Augusta Victoria (1846–1923). Married Prince Christian of Schleswig-Holstein but remained in Britain taking an active interest in a number of charities; was founding president of the Royal School of Needlework and president of the Royal British Nurses Association.

Princess Louise Caroline Alberta Marchioness of Lorne (1848–1939) Became Duchess of Argyll on her marriage to John Campbell, 9th Duke of Argyll.

Prince Arthur William Patrick Albert, Duke of Connaught and Strathearn (1850–1942). Married Princess Louise Margaret of Prussia in 1879. Served as Governor-General of Canada 1911–16.

Prince Leopold George Duncan Albert, Duke of Albany (1853–84). Married Princess Helena of Waldeck and Pyrmont in 1882. Suffered from haemophilia, which led to his death at the early age of 30.

Beatrice Mary Victoria Feodore (1857–1944). Married Prince Henry of Battenberg in 1885. Although she was very shy and suffered with rheumatism, she became well known as a regular companion of her mother.

INTO BATTLE

Richard III was the last English king to be killed in battle. He was slain at the Battle of Bosworth Field on 22 August 1485 aged 32.

The last British monarch to personally lead his troops in battle was King George II at the Battle of Dettingen in Bavaria on 27 June 1742, during the War of the Austrian Succession.

Queen Elizabeth, the Queen Mother's older brother Fergus Bowes-Lyon died of wounds he received while serving as a captain in 8th Battalion, the Black Watch in the opening stages of the Battle of Loos on 27 September 1915.

Edward VIII (abdicated before his coronation and created Duke of Windsor) was the last British monarch to be awarded a gallantry medal, a Military Cross, which he was awarded while serving as a junior officer in the Grenadier Guards on the Western Front in 1916.

Buckingham Palace's chapel, quadrangle and grounds were hit by a number of Luftwaffe bombs (incendiaries and high explosive), while King George VI and Queen Elizabeth were in residence, on 13 September 1940. The queen would later comment 'I'm glad we have been bombed. Now I can look the East End in the face.'

Prince George, Duke of Kent, the fourth son of George V, was a serving officer in the RAF when he was killed on 25 August 1942 when the Short Sunderland flying boat in which he was a passenger crashed into a hillside near Dunbeath, Caithness, in bad weather.

Queen Elizabeth II, then Princess Elizabeth, joined the Women's Auxiliary Territorial Service in February 1945, as an honorary Second Subaltern with the service number of 230873.

4

GREAT BRITONS – FAMOUS & NOT SO FAMOUS

Over the last few years a number of polls have sought the 100 greatest Britons; what follows is the author's personal selection of great Britons, NOT necessarily the *greatest*. Every one of them, however, is considered in their own way, a Great Briton. Some who enjoy enduring fame and simply have to be included, but there are many others who are sadly neglected from popular memory and those whose achievements were significant but their names remain obscure, while others are included because they exemplify and define Britishness in popular culture. They are listed in alphabetical order.

Julie Andrews (b. 1935), portrayed Mary Poppins in the film of the same name and Maria in *The Sound of Music*.

David Attenborough (b. 1926), the ultimate nature documentary presenter.

Jane Austen (1775–1817), author of such great books as *Sense and Sensibility*, *Pride and Prejudice* and *Emma*.

Charles Babbage (1791–1871), originated the concept of a programmable computer.

John Logie Baird (1888–1946), inventor of the first practical television.

Tony Benn (b. 1925), politician, true man of the people and campaigner for peace.

Alan Bennett (b. 1934), playwright, actor and author. Came to prominence with the *Beyond the Fringe* satirical review, his works on radio, television and film are diverse but capture the very essence of the British people. He is a national treasure.

John Betjeman (1906–84), much-loved poet, writer and broadcaster who captured the manners, life, loves, humour, places and emotive subjects dearest to the hearts of British people.

William Booth (1829–1912), the founder of the Salvation Army.

Richard Branson (b. 1950), entrepreneur, adventurer and business magnate.

Isambard Kingdom Brunel (1806–59), England's greatest civil engineer.

Robert Burns (1759–96), the national poet of Scotland whose works include 'Auld Lang Syne', 'Scots Wha Hae', 'Tam o'Shanter' and 'Address To a Haggis'. Burns Nights, a celebration of his birthday (25 January), are still celebrated all over the world.

Richard Burton (1821–90), explorer, cartographer, ethnologist and spy.

Richard Burton (1925–84), one of the finest stage and film actors of his day.

Michael Caine (b. 1933), actor whose iconic British character film performances include: Lieutenant Gonville Bromhead in *Zulu* (1964), Harry Palmer in *The Ipcress File* (1965), *Alfie* (1965), Charlie Croker in *The Italian Job* (1969), Jack Carter in *Get Carter* (1971), Peachy Carneham in *The Man Who Would be King* (1975) and Lieutenant Colonel John Vandeleur in *A Bridge Too Far* (1977).

Donald Campbell (1921–67), land and water speed record breaker.

Edith Cavell (1865–1915), Britain's greatest heroine of the First World War.

Winston Churchill (1874–1965), would we have won the Second World War without him?

Sean Connery (b. 1930), the original and truly iconic 007 James Bond on film.

Captain James Cook RN (1728–79), explorer, navigator and cartographer.

Peter Cook (1937–95), brilliant satirist, writer, character actor and comedian.

Henry Cooper (1934–2011), boxing legend and a true gentleman in and out of the ring. He held the British, Commonwealth and European heavyweight titles several times throughout his career.

Tommy Cooper (1921–84), affectionately remembered comedy magician.

Noël Coward (1899–1973), wit, playwright, composer, director and actor and, above all, an English gentleman.

Michael Crawford (b. 1942), versatile actor and singer best known for his portrayal of Frank Spencer in *Some Mothers Do 'Ave 'Em* and on stage in *The Phantom of the Opera*.

Quentin Crisp (1908–99), author of *The Naked Civil Servant*, in many ways he was the first flamboyant gay icon of modern times and a uniquely English gentleman.

Oliver Cromwell (1599–1658), English Civil War General, politician and eventually Lord Protector.

Charles Darwin (1809–82), author of *On the Origin of Species* (1859).

Judi Dench (b. 1934), stage, screen and television actress who has played Queen Victoria in *Mrs Brown* (1997) and has portrayed 'M' in the James Bond films since 1995.

Diana, Princess of Wales (1961–97), the People's Princess.

Charles Dickens (1809–82), author whose works captured life and society in the mid-Victorian age.

Vice-Admiral Sir Francis Drake (1540–96), circumnavigated the world and second in command of the British fleet against the Spanish Armada.

Sir Arthur Conan Doyle (1859–1930), creator of Sherlock Holmes.

James Dyson (b. 1947), inventor of the dual cyclone bagless vacuum cleaner.

Edward Elgar (1857–1934), Classical composer of quintessentially British anthems and music such as the *Enigma Variations* and the *Pomp and Circumstance Marches*. The music of Edward Elgar is integral to the Last Night of the Proms.

Queen Elizabeth I (1533–1603), her reign is regarded as a 'Golden Age' for Britain.

Queen Elizabeth II (b. 1926), dedicated and dignified monarch who has dedicated her life to her country, Commonwealth and her people for sixty years.

Queen Elizabeth, the Queen Mother (1900–2002), much-loved queen consort of King George VI.

Michael Faraday (1791–1867), discovered the magnetic field, electromagnetic induction, diamagnetism and electrolysis.

Sir Ranulph Fiennes (b. 1944), the world's greatest living explorer.

Alexander Fleming (1881–1955), discovered the antibiotic penicillin.

Ian Fleming (1908–64), creator of 007 James Bond.

Edward Fox (b. 1937), although well known for his portrayal of English upper-class characters from Lord Hugh Trimingham in *The Go-Between* (1970), Edward VIII in *Edward and Mrs Simpson* (1978) and Lieutenant General Brian Horrocks in *A Bridge Too Far* (1977), he will also be remembered for his outstanding performance in *The Day of the Jackal* (1973).

Stephen Fry (b. 1957), actor, wit, author, playwright, journalist, comedian, television presenter and all-round national treasure (he really is a remarkably modest and lovely man).

William Ewart Gladstone (1809–98), served an unsurpassed four terms as Prime Minister.

Owain Glyndŵr (*c.* 1349–*c.* 1416), Welsh ruler and the last native Welshman to hold the title Prince of Wales.

Stephen Hawking (b. 1942), theoretical physicist and cosmologist whose work is respected worldwide.

King Henry V (1386–1422), victor of the Battle of Agincourt, 1415.

King Henry VIII (1491–1547), iconic monarch with six wives.

Richard Holmes (1946–2011), soldier, gentleman and military historian who brought military history alive for the modern generation in his books and television documentaries.

Robert Hook (1635–1703), natural philosopher, polymath and architect, who has been described as 'Britain's Leonardo'.

Anthony Hopkins (b. 1937), one of the greatest living actors on stage and screen. Although he is best known for his portrayal of Hannibal Lecter in *The Silence of the Lambs*, he deserves to be remembered for his performances in such films as *84 Charring Cross Road*, *The Remains of the Day*; as Dr Frederick Treves in *The Elephant Man* and as Lieutenant-Colonel John Frost in *A Bridge Too Far*.

'Captain' W.E. Johns (1893–1968), creator and author of the 'Biggles' books.

David Jason (b. 1940), from Granville in *Open All Hours* to 'Del Boy' Trotter in *Only Fools and Horses*, Pop Larkin in *The Darling Buds of May* and Inspector Jack Frost, David remains one of Britain's most popular actors.

Edward Jenner (1749–1843), pioneer of the smallpox vaccine.

T.E. Lawrence (1888–1935), Lawrence of Arabia – distinguished soldier, author and poet.

John Lennon (1940–80), singer, songwriter and co-writer (with Paul McCartney) of so many memorable, enduring and meaningful songs.

David Livingstone (1813–73), missionary and explorer.

John Lydon (Johnny Rotten) (b. 1956), lead singer of revolutionary punk group *The Sex Pistols*.

Humphrey 'Humph' Lyttelton (1921–2008), jazz trumpeter, gentleman and the unlikely but rather wonderful chairman of BBC Radio 4's *I'm Sorry I Haven't a Clue.*

Paul McCartney (b. 1942), singer, songwriter and co-writer (with John Lennon) of so many memorable, enduring and meaningful songs.

Helen Mirren (b. 1945), acclaimed theatre, film and television actress best known for her unforgettable portrayal of Morgana in the film *Excalibur* (1981), Queen Elizabeth II in *The Queen* (2006) and as DCI Jane Tennison in the *Prime Suspect* series

Field Marshal Bernard Law Montgomery (1887–1976), victor of the Battle of El Alamein, 1942.

Bobby Moore (1941–93), captain of the victorious England World Cup-winning side of 1966.

Thomas More (1478–1535), philosopher, statesman and martyr.

Eric Morecambe (1926–84), comedian, best remembered for his long partnership with Ernie Wise and the enduring appeal of their comedy shows.

Frank Muir (1920–98), comedy writer, wit and television personality – a quintessential English gentleman.

Admiral Lord Horatio Nelson (1758–1805), Britain's greatest naval commander.

Sir Isaac Newton (1642–1727), his descriptions of universal gravitation and the three laws of motion dominated the scientific view of the physical universe for 300 years.

Florence Nightingale (1820–1910), nursing pioneer.

Captain Lawrence Oates (1880–1912), sacrificed his life to give the other members of the South Pole expedition a chance of survival. He left the tent and strode into a blizzard with the immortal words 'I am just going outside and may be some time.'

Laurence Olivier (1907–89), one of the most revered actors on stage, film and television of all time. His canon of Shakespearian performances is remarkable and iconic; his performance in the lead in the film of *Henry V* rallied Britain in 1944. He narrated the series *The World at War* (1973–4) and was one of the founders, and the inaugural director, of the National Theatre.

Michael Palin (b. 1943), member of the *Monty Python* comedy team, renowned world travel documentary maker, actor, author and one of the nicest men on British television.

Emmeline Pankhurst (1857–1928), leader of the suffragettes, she dedicated her life to the votes for women cause.

John Peel (1939–2004), the most influential DJ of his generation.

William Pitt the Younger (1759–1806), youngest Prime Minister (he was 24), an outstanding administrator who worked for efficiency and reform. He led Britain during the wars against France and Napoleon.

Harry Price (1881–1948), ghost hunter, author and one of the founders of modern psychical research.

Sir Walter Raleigh (1554–1618), writer, poet, adventurer, soldier and spy.

Sir Steve Redgrave (b. 1962), five–time gold medal winner, he is one of Britain's greatest Olympians.

Cliff Richard (b. 1940), the only singer to have had a No. 1 single in the UK in six consecutive decades.

J.K. Rowling (b. 1965), the author of the *Harry Potter* books.

Willie Rushton (1937–96), wit, satirist, comedian and actor. Co-founder of *Private Eye* and ever-popular panellist on BBC Radio 4's *I'm Sorry I Haven't a Clue*.

Captain Robert Falcon Scott RN (1868–1912), 'Scott of the Antarctic' was the explorer who lost his life during the expedition he was leading to the South Pole.

Maggie Smith (b. 1934), stage, film and screen actress who came to prominence for her lead in the television adaptation of *The Prime of Miss Jean Brodie* and is today is best known for portraying the epitome English aristocratic ladies on film and television.

Dusty Springfield (Mary Isobel Bernadette O'Brien) (1939–99), pop legend, to many she was 'The White Queen of Soul' whose enduring hits include: 'I Only Want to Be with You' (1963), 'I Just Don't Know What to Do with Myself' (1964), 'You Don't Have to Say You Love Me' (1966), and 'Son of a Preacher Man' (1968).

George Stephenson (1781–1848), 'the Father of Railways' he built the first public railway line in the world to use steam locomotives.

Marie Stopes (1880–1958), women's rights campaigner and pioneer in the field of birth control.

Ellen Terry (1847–1928), the greatest actress of her day.

Margaret Thatcher (b. 1925), first female British Prime Minister.

J.R.R. Tolkien (1892–1973), John Ronald Reuel Tolkien, author of *The Hobbit* and *The Lord of the Rings*.

Mary Tourtel (1874–1948), creator of Rupert the Bear.

Alan Turing (1912–54), Bletchley Park codebreaker – a genius who helped change the course of the war.

Queen Victoria (1819–1901), reigned for 64 years. As queen she was the epitome of Britain and her Empire.

William Wallace (*c.* 1272–1305), one of Scotland's greatest heroes, he defeated an English at the Battle of Stirling Bridge in 1297.

James Watt (1736–1819), Scottish inventor and mechanical engineer whose innovations and improvements to the steam engine provided the cornerstone for the Industrial Revolution.

Arthur Wellesley, Duke of Wellington (1769–1852), the victor of Waterloo and Britain's Prime Minister on two occasions.

John Wesley (1703–91), Christian theologian founder of the Methodist movement.

Frank Whittle (1907–96), inventor of the turbojet engine and 'the father of jet propulsion'.

Ralph Vaughan Williams (1872–1958), composer and collector of English folk songs whose canon of works includes such evocative British masterpieces as 'The Lark Ascending'; 'Fantasia on a Theme by Thomas Tallis'; 'In the Fen County' and his 'English Folk Song Suite'.

William Wilberforce (1759–1833), British leader of the movement to abolish slavery.

5

BRITAIN AT WORK

The Great British public have always been fascinated by unusual jobs as well evinced by the popularity and longevity of the television programme *What's My Line?* presented by Eamonn Andrews between 1951 and 1963. Regular panellists such as Lady Isobel Barnett, Barbara Kelly, Cyril Fletcher and David Nixon had to guess the occupation of contestants by asking questions to which the contestant could only reply with a 'yes' or a 'no' answer. The show was filled for over ten years with plenty of people employed in unusual occupations; so in the spirit of the show that was once a televisual institution, what follows is an A–Z of some of the unusual jobs that provided gainful employment for British people in the past.

Ale-Conner – The man appointed by the local manorial courts to examine beer for quality and checked measures to prevent fraud.

Bagniokeeper – Originally the keeper of a coffee house which offered Turkish baths, the term was later used to describe a brothel keeper.

Bal Maiden – A term commonly used in Cornwall and West Devon for women who worked on the surface in the mining industry dressing ore.

Cordwainer – A craftsman who made goods from quality soft leather, notably, fine shoes.

Dauber – Worked in building construction daubing the wattle panels with a clay and dung mix used to create the walls of a house between the timber framework.

Eyer – Made the holes in sewing needles (also known as a Holer).

Fossil digger – A miner of coprolite (fossilised dinosaur droppings); these would be processed and sold commercially for use as fertiliser.

Fripperer – A trader in old clothes and trinkets.

Gelder – A castrator of livestock.

Gong Farmer – Employed to empty and carry away the contents of cesspits, ashpits and outside toilets (also known as a Night Soil Man).

Higgler – An itinerant peddler who would often trade by bartering and haggling rather than using money.

Hog Jobbler – A buyer and seller of pigs.

Iron Puddler – A foundry worker who made wrought iron using the puddling process.

Jigger Turner – A job often carried out by a child who would spin the 'jigger wheel' by hand so a plate-maker or presser could shape pottery by pressing bats of clay onto plaster moulds on the jigger wheel as it rotated.

Knocker-up – Walked the streets of industrial areas with a long pole knocking on the windows and shutters of workers to rouse them for work.

Loblolly Boy – A Royal Navy term used for a young boy who would assist the ship's surgeon by fetching, carrying, cleaning and clearing up – especially after operations. It was considered the lowliest position on any ship.

Lumpman – A term used primarily in Cheshire for a man employed to oversee and control a salt pan and open pan salt works.

Matchet Mounter – Employed in the cutlery industry mounting knife blades into handles usually made from bone.

Naperer – A domestic servant, usually only found in a royal or high status household, with the specific responsibility for the washing and storage of table linen.

Oil Colour Man – Manufacturer and or mixer of pigmented paints for commercial painters (not be confused with an Oil & Colour Man who was a dealer in the victualling trade).

Osier Peeler – Stripped the bark from willow stems (osiers) preparing them for basket-weaving.

Peruker – A wig maker.

Planker – Kneaded or 'planked' the felt in the hat manufacturing process.

Quarrel Picker – A glazier.

Rully Man – A commercial cart driver.

Saggar Maker's Bottom Knocker – Was a job in the pottery industry usually carried out by a young lad who would make the base of the saggar from a lump of fireclay which he knocked into a metal ring using a wooden mallet or mawl (a saggar is a fireclay container, usually oval or round, used to protect pottery from marking by flames and smoke during firing in a bottle oven).

Skiver – Worked a specific process in the mass manufacture of boots and shoes where they used a sharp, revolving knife to pare the leather where it was to be folded.

Sucksmith – A smith who specialises in making ploughshare blades.

Throwster – Worker in the textile industry whose job was to mind the machine that twisted together strands of fibre into yarn, cotton, silk or wool.

Tripe dresser – Person who scrubs and boils the stomach lining of slaughtered oxen in preparation of it being sold by a butcher.

Try worker – A person employed at a try-works where whale blubber was converted into oil.

Underlooker – Mining official responsible for the safety of miners who would check the pit before each shift.

Vagina Maker – A maker of scabbards and sheaths.

Vamper – Worked in the manufacture of shoes making up the upper part of a boot or shoe covering the instep and sometimes extending over the toe.

Wharfinger – The owner or manager of a wharf or dock.

Wheel Tapper – Worked on railways inspecting the wheels of trains and carriages for cracks or damage by (yes, you've guessed it) tapping the wheels and listening to the ring they made.

Xylographer – an engraver of patterns and letters in wood for use in block printing.

Yatman – A gatekeeper or doorman.

Yeoman – A farmer who owned and farmed his own land (as opposed to being a tenant farmer who rented it).

Zincographer – Worked in the printing industry etching zinc plates for printing blocks.

6

THAT'S ENTERTAINMENT

LOCATION, LOCATION, LOCATION

Some classic films and their Great British locations

Harry Potter's Hogwarts School is created from a number of historic locations including: Lacock Abbey in Wiltshire; Harrow Boarding School; the Bodelian Library, Oxford; Gloucester Cathedral, Durham Cathedral; Christ Church Oxford and Alnwick Castle, Northumberland.

In *Carry on Up the Khyber* (1968), the scenes on the Khyber Pass were actually shot on the Watkin Path, on Mount Snowdon.

Barbara Windsor's famous pinging bra scene in *Carry on Camping* (1969) was filmed in The Orchard, Pinewood Studios, Buckinghamshire.

The Long Hampton Hospital in *Carry on Doctor* (1967) and *Carry on Again Doctor* (1969) was actually Maidenhead Town Hall in Berkshire.

The exterior barrack scenes in *Carry on Sergeant* (1958) were filmed at Queens Barracks, Stoughton, Surrey.

Although most of the exteriors for the *Dad's Army* television series were filmed around Thetford in Norfolk, the film *Dad's Army* (1971) was shot in the village and surrounding area of Chalfont St Giles in Buckinghamshire.

Many of the scenes in *Chitty Chitty Bang Bang* (1968) were filmed in Hambleden (the smock windmill) and at Turville in High Wycombe, Buckinghamshire.

PC George Dixon (Jack Warner) had his Dock Green police station in *The Blue Lamp* (1950) filmed at Brent Street, Hendon, London.

In *Hot Fuzz* (2007) starring Simon Pegg and Nick Frost, Wells in Somerset became the fictional town of Sandiford.

In *Alfie* (1966), Michael Caine's seedy bedsit was filmed at 29 St Stephen's Gardens off Chepstow Road, Notting Hill Gate, London.

Gosford Park (2002) – Wrotham Park, Barnet (exterior and some interiors) and Syon House, Brentford (interiors).

Brief Encounter (1945) starring Trevor Howard and Celia Johnson was filmed at Carnforth station, Lancashire.

Filming for *The Titfield Thunderbolt* (1953) was largely carried out on the recently closed Bristol and North Somerset Railway branch line, formerly part of the Great Western Railway, along the Cam Brook valley between Camerton and Limpley Stoke. Titfield station was in reality Monkton Combe station, while the village of Titfield itself was nearby Freshford.

Swallows and Amazons (1974) was filmed in the Lake District National Park, at the actual locations used by Arthur Ransome to create the fictional lake in his novel of the same name.

The Go-Between (1970) starring Julie Christie and Alan Bates had filming centred around Melton Constable Hall in Norfolk but used many other locations in the county including Heydon, Thornage, Hickling Broad and Tombland in Norwich.

Batman Begins (2005) used Mentmore Towers in Buckinghamshire for the exterior shots of Wayne Manor.

The final scene of Kubrick's *Full Metal Jacket* was filmed at Beckton Gas Works, London.

Withnail and I (1986) used locations in Notting Hill, London; Sleddale Hall, Penrith, Cumbria; Tavistock Crescent, Kensington and Stony Stratford, Milton Keynes, Buckinghamshire.

In *Carry on Cowboy* (1965) Chobham Common in Woking, Surrey, had to double for the Wild West.

The exterior pier scenes in *Carry on Girls* (1973) were filmed on the West Pier, Brighton.

Calendar Girls (2003). The village hall at Kettlewell, Yorkshire, was used as a location for the meetings of Rylstone WI.

In *Out of Africa* (1985) starring Robert Redford and Meryl Streep, Castle Rising in Norfolk was turned into Denmark.

The exteriors of the buildings of the fictional Brookfield School in *Goodbye, Mr Chips* (1939) were filmed at Repton School, Derbyshire.

The iconic 'You were only supposed to blow the bloody doors off' scene in *The Italian Job* (1969) was filmed at the old motor racing circuit at Crystal Palace.

The underground car park, in which Macleod (Christopher Lambert) decapitates a rival immortal in the opening scenes of *Highlander* (1986) was filmed in the Earl's Court underground car park in London.

Much of the film *The Railway Children*, starring Jenny Agutter, was filmed in West Yorkshire. The famous 'Daddy! My Daddy!' scene was filmed on Oakworth station on the preserved Keighley & Worth Valley Railway.

The RAF base scenes for *Reach for the Sky* (1956) starring Kenneth More were filmed at RAF Kenley, Surrey.

In Spielberg's *Saving Private Ryan* (1998) all scenes involving street fighting in and around towns and the final battle scene were all filmed in Hatfield, Hertfordshire.

When Gwyneth Paltrow walks along a tropical island shore in the final scene of *Shakespeare in Love* (1998), she is actually walking along Holkham beach in Norfolk.

In *Quadrophenia* (1979), the spectacular white cliffs from which Jimmy (Phil Daniels) ultimately takes a dive on Ace's jazzed-up scooter are at Beachy Head, south-west of Eastbourne.

In *The Prime of Miss Jean Brodie* (1969), starring Maggie Smith, the school used for the filming was Donaldson's School for the Deaf, Henderson Row, Edinburgh.

During the filming of *Die Another Day* (2002) starring Pierce Brosnan as James Bond, farmland at Burnham Deepdale in Norfolk was turned into a North Korean paddy field.

The beach used for the iconic running scenes in *Chariots of Fire* (1981) was West Sands, St Andrew's, and the Olympic Stadium was the Bebington Oval, Merseyside.

In *Bridget Jones's Diary* (2001), her flat was above the Globe public house on Borough High Street, London.

The first werewolf attack scenes in *An American Werewolf in London* (1981) were filmed in Windsor Great Park in Berkshire.

In the Ealing classic *The Ladykillers* (1955), Mrs Wilberforce's house was a set built at the western end of Frederica Street, directly above the southern portal of Copenhagen Tunnel on the railway line leading out of King's Cross railway station.

The dramatic train sequences in the James Bond films *Octopussy* (1983) and *Goldeneye* (1995) were filmed on the Nene Valley Railway, Cambridgeshire.

The climactic scenes of *Mission: Impossible* (1996) starring Tom Cruise on the 'cross-channel' railway were filmed in Scotland, on stretches of line between Annan and Dumfries.

In *Monty Pyton and the Holy Grail* (1975) the taunting of King Arthur and his knights by the French with such exclamations as 'I fart in your general direction!' and 'Your mother was a hamster and your father smelt of elderberries!' at Guy de Loimbard's castle was filmed at Doune Castle, Stirling.

The famous nude wresting scene between Oliver Reed and Alan Bates in Ken Russell's film adaptation of D.H. Lawrence's *Women in Love* was filmed at Elvaston Castle in Derbyshire.

Some of the more revealing scenes of *The Full Monty* (1997) starring Robert Carlyle were filmed in the Shiregreen Working Men's Club, Sheffield.

The opening scenes of *A Hard Day's Night* (1964) where The Beatles run along a railway platform pursued by fans, supposedly on Liverpool Lime Street station, was actually filmed at London's Marylebone station.

In Which We Serve (1942) starring Noël Coward and John Mills was filmed at Plymouth in Devon and Portland in Dorset.

The exterior of Dr Phibes's mansion in *The Abominable Dr Phibes* (1971) starring Vincent Price was Immanuel College, Elstree, Hertfordshire.

The exterior locations for *Blythe Spirit* (1945) starring Rex Harrison, were in the village of Denham, Buckinghamshire, where the Condomine house was 'Fairway' on Cheapside Lane.

The haunting image of Meryl Streep standing on a windswept sea wall in *The French Lieutenant's Woman* (1981) was filmed on the Cobb at Lyme Regis, Dorset.

Billy Elliot (2000) was filmed in and around Easington, County Durham.

In *Get Carter* (1971) the 'Las Vegas Boarding House' where Jack Carter (Michael Caine) stayed was on Coburg Street in Gateshead.

Under Milk Wood (1973), starring Richard Burton, Elizabeth Taylor and Peter O'Toole, was filmed in Lower Town, Fishguard, Pembrokeshire.

The scenes at the golf club in the Sean Connery, James Bond classic *Goldfinger* (1964) were filmed at Stoke Poges Golf Club, Berkshire.

In the James Bond film *The World Is Not Enough* (1999) starring Pierce Brosnan, the MI6 HQ 'Castle Thane' is Eilean Donan Castle, Dornie, Scotland.

Pride and Prejudice (2005) – Wilton House, Salisbury, Wiltshire; Martin Down Nature Reserve, Hampshire; Burghley House, Stamford, Lincolnshire; Chatsworth House, Derbyshire; and Basildon Park, Reading, Berkshire.

Yanks (1979), starring Richard Gere, was filmed extensively in the village of Uppermill, Cheshire.

The school used for the main set in *Kes* (1969) was St Helens School, Athersley South, now renamed Edward Sheerin School, Barnsley.

In *The Thirty-Nine Steps* (1979) the dramatic scene where Richard Hannay (Robert Powell) bails out and clings to the Forth Bridge were filmed on the Severn Valley Railway and the Victoria Bridge over the River Severn at Arley.

Despite being set in Edinburgh, almost all of Danny Boyle's adaptation of Irving Welsh's *Trainspotting (1996)* was filmed in Glasgow.

In the film *The Eagle has Landed* (1977), the 'Norfolk village' of Studley Constable was actually Mapledurham in Berkshire.

Frank N. Furter's castle in *The Rocky Horror Picture Show* (1975) was Oakley Court Hotel, Windsor, Berkshire.

The majority of the exterior filming for *Saturday Night and Sunday Morning* (1960) starring Albert Finney and Shirley Anne Field was shot around Nottingham.

The castle scenes in the Walt Disney children's classic *Bedknobs and Broomsticks* (1971) were shot at Corfe Castle in Dorset.

The village seen in the camera obscura in *A Matter of Life and Death* (1946) starring David Niven and Kim Hunter, was Shere in Surrey.

The exterior shots for *Carry on Matron* (1972) were filmed at Heatherwood Hospital, Ascot.

In *Robin Hood, Prince of Thieves* (1991), Robin (Kevin Costner) and Azeem (Morgan Freeman) land in England upon the beach at Seven Sisters, Eastbourne, East Sussex.

Both *The Battle of Britain* (1969) and *Memphis Belle* (1990) had numerous scenes filmed upon Duxford Airfield, Cambridgeshire.

The Village of the Damned (1960) known as Midwich, was Letchmore Heath, Hertfordshire.

Brighton Rock (1947), starring Richard Attenborough, was indeed filmed around Brighton, including Church Street, Little East Street (Star and Garter pub), North Lane, Palace Pier and The Lanes.

The Ealing comedy *Whisky Galore!* (1948) was shot almost entirely on the Scottish island of Barra.

Billy Liar (1963) starring Julie Christie and Tom Courtney was mostly filmed around Bradford and West Yorkshire. The dance hall, where Billy's romantic entanglements caught up with him, was the Bradford Locarno.

Whistle Down the Wind (1961) starring Hayley Mills, Bernard Lee and Alan Bates was filmed at Downham in Lancashire.

In the *Wicker Man* (1973) starring Edward Woodward and Christopher Lee, the wicker man itself was built on the Machars Peninsula, between Luce and Wigtown Bays, south of Newton Stewart in Dumfries and Galloway.

SOME AFFECTIONATELY REMEMBERED BRITISH CHILDREN'S TELEVISION PROGRAMMES

Andy Pandy first appeared as part of *For the Children* (later *Watch with Mother*) on the BBC in 1950.

There are only thirteen episodes of *Bagpuss* originally run from 12 February to 7 May 1974. At the beginning of each episode Emily would bring a broken item to the toy shop to be mended and recite the words:

> Bagpuss, dear Bagpuss
> Old Fat Furry Catpuss
> Wake up and look at this thing that I bring
> Wake up, be bright, be golden and light
> Bagpuss, oh hear what I sing

Once Emily had left, the toys would magically come to life, discuss and mend the item, then, when all was done, Bagpuss would yawn, the colour faded to sepia and the toys would return to being toys again.

Basil Brush first appeared on British television in 1963. In the 1970s Basil was regularly accompanied by Mr Roy (Roy North) and Mr Derek (Derek Fowlds).

Blue Peter was first aired in 1958 and is the world's longest-running children's television show.

The Welsh language version of *Bob the Builder* is called *Bob Y Bildar* and began airing on S4C in October 2006

Although there were only 13 episodes, *Bod* ran from 1975 to 1984 and featured the voices of John Le Mesurier and Maggie Henderson.

Camberwick Green originally appeared in 1966 and featured such characters as Windy Miller, Roger Varley the chimney sweep, PC McGarry number 452 and Captain Snort of Pippin Fort.

Captain Pugwash made his debut in a comic strip format in the first issue of *The Eagle* in 1950. He first appeared on BBC television in 1957 and in a colour series first shown in 1974–5.

Catweazle, played by Geoffrey Bayldon and first shown on ITV in 1970, was the story of an eleventh-century wizard who accidentally travelled through time to the year 1969.

'It's Friday, It's five o'clock . . .' The presenters of *Crackerjack* were Eamonn Andrews (1955–64), Leslie Crowther (1964–8), Michael Aspel (1968–74), Ed Stewart (1975–9) and Stu Francis (1980–4).

Fingerbobs consisted of 13 episodes first shown in 1972. The presenter, Mr Yoffy, was Canadian actor and musician Rick Jones and featured the finger puppets Fingermouse, a mouse; Gulliver, a seagull; Scampi . . . er . . . the scampi and Flash, a tortoise.

The ITV children's educational programme *How* first appeared in 1966 and was originally presented solo by Jack Hargreaves. He was soon joined by the regular team of Fred Dinenage (1966–81), Jon Miller (1966–81), Bunty James (1966–9 and 1970–6), Dr Tom Gaskell (1969), Jill Graham (1969–70) and Marian Davies (1977–81).

Ivor the Engine was created and narrated by Oliver Postgate. It first appeared in black and white in 1959 with a later colour series of forty 5-minute episodes first aired between 1975 and 1977.

Jackanory was first transmitted on 13 December 1965 and ran to over 3,000 episodes over the next thirty years. The story tellers include: Margaret Rutherford, Hattie Jacques, Joyce Grenfell, Willie Rushton, Tom Baker, Peter Sellers, Alfred Marks, John Grant reading his own '*Littlenose*' stories, Kenneth Williams, Bernard Holley reading the Jonny Briggs stories by Joan Eadington and Bernard Cribbins – the master of children's storytelling who appeared on a total of 114 programmes.

Larry the Lamb first appeared as a character in the *Toytown* radio series for children written by S.G. Hulme Beaman, first broadcast by the BBC in 1929.

In the fantasy series *Lizzie Dripping* originally aired from 1973 to 1975, Lizzie was played by future *Blue Peter* presenter Tina Heath.

There are just thirteen 15-minute episodes of *Mr Benn,* first shown on the BBC in 1971 and 1972. They are: The Red Knight, The Big Game Hunter, The Cook, The Caveman, The Balloonist, The Zoo Keeper, The Diver, The Wizard, The Cowboy, The Clown, The Magic Carpet, The Spaceman and The Pirate. The Gladiator episode was made over thirty years later in 2005.

The *Mr Men* began as books by Roger Hargreaves first published in 1971. The first television series, consisting of a total of 28 episodes was produced in 1974 and narrated by *Dad's Army* star Arthur Lowe.

Paddington Bear first appeared in children's books written by Michael Bond, published in 1958. The BBC TV series *Paddington*, narrated by Michael Hordern, was first broadcast in 1975.

Pipkins, featuring the puppets Hartley Hare, Pig, Tortoise, Topov the Monkey and Octavia the Ostrich, ran from January 1973 to December 1981.

Play Away ran from 1971 until 1984 with such wonderful presenters as Brian Cant, Carol Chell, Toni Arthur, Derek Griffiths, Floella Benjamin, Chloe Ashcroft and even occasional appearances by Tony Robinson, Anita Dobson and Jeremy Irons.

Play School ran from April 1964 until March 1988 and originally appeared on weekday mornings on BBC2. The original line-up of toys on the show were: Big Ted; Little Ted; Jemima the rag doll; Hamble, a (pretty ugly) plastic doll and Humpty, a soft toy reminiscent of the nursery rhyme character Humpty Dumpty. A rocking horse named Dapple was also seen in a number of episodes. A segment of each episode of *Play School* would contain a short film about people at work or play, factories or animals – but before it was shown viewing children would be asked to guess whether they would see it through either the round, square, or arched window. *Play School* presenters include a number of those who appeared on *Play Away*, such as Brian Cant, Derek Griffiths, Carol Chell and Floella Benjamin but there were also appearances by Fred Harris, Carol Leader, Iain Lauchlan, Stuart McGugan, Sheelagh Gilbey, Colin Jeavons, Johnny Ball, Eric Thompson and Phyllida Law.

Postman Pat was first shown as a 13-episode series on BBC1 in 1981. The charming stories relate the gentle adventures of Pat Clifton, a postman, and his black and white cat named Jess. The series is set in the fictional village of Greendale that was inspired by the real valley of Longsleddale in Cumbria.

The ITV children's show *Rainbow* ran for more than 1,000 episodes from October 1972 until it was cancelled in March 1992. The original presenter was David Cook, but best remembered is Geoffrey Hayes along with his bear-suited housemate Bungle and the puppets George the camp pink hippo and Zippy, voiced and operated by Peter Hawkins, then operated by Ronnie Le Drew and voiced by Roy Skelton. Both Peter and Roy were also well known for voicing Daleks and Cybermen in *Doctor Who*. Another regular feature of Rainbow were the musical performers Rod, Jane and Freddy. Originally known as Rod, Matt and Jane when they debuted on the show in 1974, the group comprised Rod Burton, Jane Tucker and Matthew Corbett (later of *The Sooty Show* fame). Corbett left the trio in 1976 and was replaced by Roger Walker. When Roger left in 1980 he was replaced by Freddy Marks. Rod and Jane had been married, they divorced and Jane later got together with Freddy (crikey).

BBC TV children's comedy series *Rentaghost* ran from 1976 to 1984. The original ghosts were: Timothy Claypole, a medieval jester (Michael Staniforth); Fred Mumford (Anthony Jackson), a young man afraid to tell his parents that he was dead; Hubert Davenport (Michael Darbyshire) a Regency dandy, and not forgetting show stalwarts, the long-suffering neighbours Harold and Ethel Meaker (Edward Bradshaw and Ann Emery).

One of the most surreal game shows for kids on the slightly more edgy ITV children's programme schedule during the 1970s and early '80s was *Runaround* presented by Mike Reid – a man best known for his adult comedy act.

Sooty is a much-loved British institution. *The Sooty Show* was devised and presented by Harry Corbett and was first aired on the BBC in 1955. However, it is a little-known fact that Harry Corbett was a nephew of legendary fish and chip shop chain owner Harry Ramsden.

Teletubbies mesmerised pre-school children between 1997 and 2002 and was narrated by Tim Whitnall, Toyah Willcox, Eric Sykes and Rolf Saxon.

The Clangers, created by Oliver Postgate, consists of 26 episodes and one special shown between 1969 and 1974. The principal characters were Granny Clanger, Major Clanger, Mother Clanger, Small Clanger and Tiny Clanger who lived on a hollow planet, far, far away, nourished by Blue String Pudding, and Green Soup harvested from the planet's volcanic soup wells by the Soup Dragon.

Bill and Ben were The Flower Pot Men, first transmitted on the BBC as a segment of *Watch with Mother* in 1952.

The Flumps, broadcast on numerous occasions between 1976 and 1988, was the story of the little round furry extended family of Grandpa, Father and Mother Flump and their children Posie, Perkin and little Pootle. It was narrated by the wonderful Gay Soper and had a memorable theme tune played on the trombone by jazz musician George Chisholm.

The Wombles was a phenomenon of children's television made between 1973 and 1975, narrated by Bernard Cribbins. Pioneers in recycling the rubbish they found on Wimbledon Common, regular characters in the programme included Great Uncle Bulgaria, Tobermory, Orinoco, Bungo, Tomsk, Wellington and Madame Cholet.

The Woodentops was first shown on the BBC in 1955. The Woodentop family consisted of Daddy, Mummy, their twin children Jenny and Willy and Baby, with other characters including Spotty Dog, Buttercup the Cow, Sam Scrubbitt and Mrs Scrubbitt.

Tiswas, officially claimed to be an acronym standing for 'Today is Saturday, Watch and Smile', was an ITV Saturday morning show that ran from January 1974 to April 1982 with Chris Tarrant as anchor presenter and Sally James who joined the show as its first female presenter in 1977. In those later, golden years, appearances were made by Lenny Henry, Bob Carolgees and Spit the Dog, Frank Carson, Norman Collier and Fogwell Flax, and not forgetting the Phantom Flan Flinger!

Trumpton was narrated by Brian Cant and was originally run from January to March 1967. The inspiration for the name is believed to have stemmed from the East Sussex village of Wivelsfield Green, supported by the nearby villages of Plumpton (Trumpton) and Chailey (Chigley). Trumpton was the county town of Trumptonshire and the show told the story of daily life in the town. The most memorable feature of every episode was Captain Flack's roll-call for the Trumpton Fire Brigade: 'Pugh, Pugh, Barney McGrew, Cuthbert, Dibble, Grub.'

Chigley is the story of the village of Chigley, near Camberwick Green in Trumptonshire, originally shown between October and December 1969. Chigley's main employer is a biscuit factory that releases its staff promptly at 6 o'clock when a whistle sounds the end of the day's work. The employees are fortunate to have the benevolent Lord Belborough who extends an invitation to everyone to join him in the gardens of Winkstead Hall where his lordship plays his vintage Dutch organ and the locals dance together as the episodes come to an end.

Vision On, a BBC1 favourite from 1964 to 1976, was actually designed specifically for deaf children. The main presenters were actress Pat Keysell, who also taught children with hearing difficulties; with her was the wonderful artist Tony Hart, the mime artists Ben Benison and Sylvester McCoy, the eccentric inventor Wilf Lunn and the author's personal favourite, David Cleveland who appeared in short film skits as the Prof. One thing that really lingers in the memory about *Vision On* is the music. The opening titles were 'Accroche-Toi, Caroline' by Caravelli, recorded by the Paris Studio Group. The original gallery theme was 'Cavatina' but the later gallery theme 'Left Bank Two' by Wayne Hill (recorded by the Noveltones) is the one most recall with affection. Then there was that closing theme, a gem called 'Java', as recorded by Al Hirt and Bert Kaempfert.

Worzel Gummidge, a walking, talking scarecrow with interchangeable heads (that part was always a bit scary), originally appeared in a series of children's books by Barbara Euphan Todd published between 1936 and 1963. Worzel came to the television screens in an ITV series in 1979 with John Pertwee as Worzel, Una Stubbs as lifesize fairground doll Aunt Sally and Geoffrey 'Catweazle' Bayldon as the Crowman, the man who made Worzel and some of his other scarecrow friends.

FIFTEEN GREAT CLASSIC TV ADVERTS AND STRAP LINES

'John Collier – The window to watch' (High Street clothing retailer)

'For Mash Get Smash' (Powdered mashed potato)

'Ahhhhhhhh . . . Bisto' (Gravy)

'And all because the lady loves, Milk Tray' (Cadbury's chocolates)

'Do the Shake n' Vac and put the freshness back' (carpet freshener)

'Watch out! There's a Humphrey about!' (Unigate milk)

'It's frothy man!' (Cresta fizzy drinks)

'Everyone's a fruit and nutcase' (Cadbury's chocolate bar)

'It looks good, it tastes good, and by golly it does you good' (Mackeson Beer)

'A finger of fudge is just enough to give your kids a treat' (Cadbury's chocolate bar)

'I'm a secret lemonade drinker' (R. White's lemonade)

'Dum, Dum, Dum, Dum, Esso Blue' (paraffin oil)

'This is the age . . . of the train' (British Rail)

'You're never alone with a Strand' (cigarettes)

'Murray Mints, Murray Mints, the too good to hurry mints' (sweets)

LISTEN TO THE BANNED

Ten records that were, rather surprisingly, originally banned by the BBC:

'God Bless the Child' – Billie Holiday (1942)
'Paper Doll' – The Mills Brothers (1943)
'Don't Let's Be Beastly to the Germans' – Noël Coward (1943)
'The Christening' – Arthur Askey (1943)
'Rum and Coca-Cola' – The Andrews Sisters (1945)
'The Deck of Cards' – T. Texas Tyler (1948)
'Somebody Up There Likes Me' – Perry Como (1956)
'Bewitched, Bothered and Bewildered' – Ella Fitzgerald (1958)
'Mack the Knife' – Bobby Darin (1959)
'Ebony Eyes' – The Everly Brothers (1961)

TEN GREAT BRITISH CLASSICAL COMPOSERS

Benjamin Britten (1913–76), the composer of *Peter Grimes*, *A Midsummer Night's Dream,* 'The Young Person's Guide to the Orchestra' and 'War Requiem'. Britten also composed the musical arrangement for the poem specially written by W.H. Auden for the 1936 film *Night Mail*.

George Butterworth (1885–1916), best known for his orchestral idyll 'The Banks of Green Willow' and his song settings of poems of A.E. Housman.

Eric Coates (1886–1957), composer of light orchestral music notably 'By the Sleepy Lagoon' (1930) the irreplaceable theme for *Desert Island Discs*. Coates, however, will be best remembered for his title theme for the film *The Dam Busters* (1954).

Frederick Delius (1862–1934), famous for his sublimely atmospheric orchestral work 'On Hearing the First Cuckoo in Spring' and 'Brigg Fair', a beautiful orchestral rhapsody based on an old English folk song.

Edward Elgar (1857–1934), the composer of such quintessentially British masterpieces as the *Enigma Variations* and the *Pomp and Circumstance Marches*.

Hubert Parry (1848–1918), composer of music for the choral song 'Jerusalem' (the words were by William Blake) and the coronation anthem 'I was Glad' composed for Edward VII and revised to include the now familiar introduction for the coronation of George V in 1911.

Henry Purcell (1659–95), composer of uniquely English baroque music. Among many wonderful pieces he composed an anthem and two elegies for Queen Mary II's funeral.

Arthur Sullivan (1842–1900) and **W.S. Gilbert** (1836–1911), respectively, the composer and librettist were creators of such typically British comic operas as *HMS Pinafore*, *The Pirates of Penzance*, *Trial by Jury* and *Iolanthe*.

William Walton (1902–83), prolific composer best and most affectionately remembered for his *Spitfire Prelude and Fugue* from his score for the film *The First of the Few* (1942).

Ralph Vaughan Williams (1872–1958), composer and collector of English folk songs, his wonderfully British works include 'The Lark Ascending'; 'Fantasia on a Theme by Thomas Tallis', 'In the Fen County' and his 'English Folk Song Suite'.

SOME MAESTROS OF BRITISH FILM AND TV THEMES

Monty Norman (b. 1928), the James Bond theme.

John Barry (1933–2011), scored *Dr No* and worked on eleven out of the next fourteen James Bond films including *Goldfinger* (1964), *Thunderball* (1965), *You Only Live Twice* (1967) and *On Her Majesty's Secret Service* (1969), as well as the title theme for the TV show *The Persuaders* starring Roger Moore and Tony Curtis.

Alan Hawkshaw (b. 1937), the Dave Allen theme, *Arthur C. Clark's Mysterious World*, the 'Chimes' jingle on Channel 4's *Countdown*, *Grandstand* and composed the music 'The Night Rider' used on the Cadbury's Milk Tray adverts.

Edwin Astley (1922–98), *The Champions*, the title music for *The Adventures of Robin Hood*, *Danger Man*, *The Saint*, *Return of the Saint*, *Department S* and *Randall and Hopkirk (Deceased)*.

Laurie Johnson (b. 1927), the theme tune used for theme for *Top Secret* (entitled 'Sucu Sucu'), *This is Your Life* (entitled 'Gala Performance'), *The Avengers* (from 1965), *Animal Magic* (piece entitled 'Las Vegas'), *Jason King* and the theme for *The Professionals*.

Ron Goodwin (1925–2003), *Where Eagles Dare, Battle of Britain, 633 Squadron, Those Magnificent Men in their Flying Machines, Monte Carlo or Bust, Operation Crossbow, Force 10 from Navarone, One of Our Dinosaurs is Missing*, a number of the Miss Marple films starring Margaret Rutherford and the BBC Radio 4 panel game *I'm Sorry I Haven't A Clue*.

Tony Hatch (b. 1939), *Crossroads, Emmerdale, Man Alive, Mr & Mrs* and *Ghost Squad*.

John Addison (1920–98), *A Bridge Too Far*.

Eric Rogers (1921–81), *Sunday Night at the London Palladium, No Sex Please: We're British* and many of the Carry On films.

Denis King (b. 1939), *The Adventures of Black Beauty* (did it make you cry every time?), *Worzel Gummidge* and *Lovejoy*.

Barry Gray (1908–84), *The Adventures of Twizzle, Torchy the Battery Boy, Fireball XL5, Stingray, Thunderbirds, Joe 90, Captain Scarlet and the Mysterons, UFO* and *Space: 1999*.

Although born in Australia, the contribution of **Ron Grainer** (1922–81) to British television themes is immense and he did spend the majority of his professional life in Great Britain. His catalogue includes the themes for *That Was the Week That Was, Man in a Suitcase, The Prisoner, Maigret, Steptoe and Son* (entitled 'Old Ned'), *Tales of the Unexpected* and he collaborated with the BBC Radiophonic Workshop on the original theme for *Dr Who*.

TEN GREAT BRITISH AUTHORS OF THE VICTORIAN AGE

Charles Dickens (1812–70), writer and social commentator, author of *Oliver Twist* (1838), *A Christmas Carol* (1843), *David Copperfield* (first published as a novel in 1850) and *Great Expectations* (1861) among others.

William Makepeace Thackeray (1811–63), novelist and satirist, author of *Vanity Fair* (1847), a wry comment on Victorian society, its manners and morals.

Sisters **Anne, Charlotte** and **Emily Brontë** were a remarkable trio of writers. Charlotte enjoyed the first success with her novel *Jane Eyre* in 1847, closely followed by Emily with her masterpiece *Wuthering Heights* published later that same year. Anne, the youngest Brontë sister, followed in 1848 with her second and by far most successful novel, *The Tenant of Wildfell Hall*.

Best known under her pen name of **George Eliot** (she used a male pen name, she said, to ensure her works would be taken seriously), Mary Anne Evans (1819–80) wrote such classics as *Adam Bede* (1859), *The Mill on the Floss* (1860), *Silas Marner* (1861) and *Middlemarch* (1871–2).

Sir Arthur Conan Doyle (1859–1930), the creator of the Sherlock Holmes stories.

Thomas Hardy (1840–1928), author of such classics as *Far from the Madding Crowd* (1874), *The Mayor of Casterbridge* (1886) and *Tess of the d'Urbervilles* (1891).

H.G. (Herbert George) Wells (1866–1946), considered by many to be 'the father of science fiction'. His remarkable and enduring canon of works includes: *The Time Machine* (1895), *The Island of Doctor Moreau* (1896), *The Invisible Man* (1897), *The War of the Worlds* (1898), *The First Men in the Moon* (1901) and *The Shape of Things to Come* (1933).

Sir Thomas Henry Hall Caine (1853–1931), the first man to sell a million books in Britain. All but forgotten today, his books include *The Deemster* (1887), *The Manxman* (1894) and *The Christian* (1897).

TEN WONDERFUL BRITISH CHILDREN'S BOOKS

Alice's Adventures in Wonderland by Lewis Carroll (1865)
Black Beauty by Anna Sewell (1877)
The Tale of Peter Rabbit by Beatrix Potter (1902)
Swallows and Amazons by Arthur Ransome (1930)
Moonfleet by J. Meade Falkner (1898)
Tom Brown's Schooldays by Thomas Hughes (1857)
Treasure Island by Robert Louis Stevenson (1883)
Kidnapped by Robert Louis Stevenson (1886)
The Secret Garden by Frances Hodgson Burnett (1911)
The Wind in the Willows by Kenneth Grahame (1908)

TEN GREAT BRITISH PAINTERS

Sir Joshua Reynolds (1723–92), idealised the imperfect on a grand scale.

George Stubbs (1724–1806), master of equine art.

Thomas Gainsborough (1727–88), originator (with Richard Wilson) of the eighteenth-century British landscape school.

William Blake (1757–1827), visionary artist of the Romantic Age. One of his greatest works were his illustrations for Dante's *Divine Comedy*.

John Crome (1768–1821), founder of the Norwich School of Painters.

Joseph Mallord William Turner (1775–1851), 'The Painter of Light:' he paved the way for Impressionism.

John Constable (1776–1837), captured the British landscape, best known for his paintings *Dedham Vale* (1802) and *The Hay Wain* (1821).

John Everett Millais (1829–96), one of the founders and leading lights of the Pre-Raphaelite Brotherhood.

William Morris (1834–96), textile designer and artist associated with both the Pre-Raphaelite Brotherhood and the English Arts and Crafts Movement.

Laurence Stephen Lowry (1887–1976), painted scenes of life in the industrial North, inhabiting them with his 'matchstick men'.

TEN INFLUENTIAL BRITISH MODERN ARTISTS

Henry Moore (1898–1986), a master of the semi-abstract monumental bronze sculpture.

Stanley Spencer (1891–1959), influential early modernist painter and war artist, whose original style has inspired a number of notable artists.

Francis Bacon (1909–92), original, challenging, bold, graphic and emotionally raw imagery.

Lucian Freud (1922–2011), challenged and explored the relationship between artist and model.

David Hockney (b. 1937), important contributor to the Pop Art movement of the 1960s.

Grayson Perry (b. 1960), pushes the parameters of expression and artistic narrative pottery.

Tracey Emin (b. 1963), one of the Young British Artists famous for her *My Bed* installation, consisting of her own unmade dirty bed.

Damien Hirst (b. 1965), came to prominence with his creations using dead animals in formaldehyde.

SOME BEST LOVED BRITISH POETRY

The love and affection for British poetry can be crushed out of us by over-bearing English Literature teachers and enforced study while at school and college, but some poems are wonderful expressions of the human condition, with observations of life, nature and the glory of our language. Without some old prat wittering on about what you should 'see' in the poem, you might just want to try reading these:

'If' by Rudyard Kipling

'The Old Vicarage, Grantchester' by Rupert Brooke

'I Wandered Lonely as a Cloud' otherwise known as 'Daffodils' by William Wordsworth

'Shall I compare theee to a summer's day? (Sonnet 18) by William Shakespeare

And lastly, but by no means least, a favourite of P.G. Wodehouse's Jeeves – 'Abou Ben Adhem' by James Henry Leigh Hunt

7

FOOD & DRINK

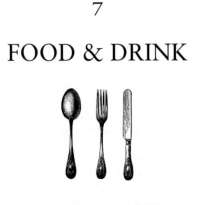

BRITISH BANGERS!

It is believed that sausages were brought to Britain by the Romans some time before AD 400.

According to the *Oxford English Dictionary*, the first specific reference in English was in a fifteenth-century vocabulary that noted 'Salcicia', a 'sawsage'.

There are more than 470 recipes and flavours for sausages in Britain.

On any given day, an estimated 5 million Britons will eat sausages.

During the year to June 2011 the British public consumed 191,040 tonnes of sausages. Laid end to end this would provide enough chipolatas to form a wall, four sausages high, around the entire coastline of Great Britain!

The world's longest sausage (at the time), weighing in at a massive 15.5 tonnes and measured to be 35 miles long, was made during British Sausage Week in 2000.

There is even a British Sausage Appreciation Society that boasts some 5,000 members.

SOME GREAT BRITISH SAUSAGES

Aberdeen Sausage (Scotland)
Beef Cervelat (England and Scotland)
Beef Sausage (Scotland)
Black Pots (Cornwall)
Blood and Tongue (England)
Bonnachen (Scotland)
Cambridge Sausage (England)
Celebrated Newmarket Sausage (Suffolk)
Checkett's Ombersley Gold Award Sausage (Worcestershire)
Deer Pudding (Scotland)
Edwards Merguez (Wales)
Maunder's Devon Chunky (England)
Biggles Marylebone Pork (England)
Muff's Old English (Wirral, Merseyside)
Epping Sausage (England)
Fish Sausage (England and Scotland)
Gloucester Sausage (England)
Kentish Sausage (England)
Lincolnshire Sausage (England)
Crombie's Lucifer's Matchsticks (Edinburgh)
Malmesbury King (Wiltshire, England)
Manchester Sausage (England)
Mettrick's High Peak Hoggett (Derbyshire)
Mutton Sausage (West Country, England)
Oxford Sausage (England)
Papworth's Champion Sausage (Norfolk)
Pink's Cumberland Sausage (Cumbria)
Pwdin Gwaed (Wales)
Rothbury's Cragside Cracker (Northumberland)
Saster (Scotland)
Suffolk Sausage (England)
The Far-famed Bury (Lancashire)
The North Staffordshire (Staffordshire)
The Stretford (England)
The Yorkshire (England)
Tunbridge Wells Sausage (England)
Upton's Hampshire Specials (England)
Wiltshire Sausage (England)
Yorkshire Sausage (England)

TRADITIONAL FOODS OF WALES

Bara Brith ('Mottled Bread'), a classic tea cake incorporating fruit and spices.

Cawl Cennin (Leek Broth).

Caws Pob (Welsh Rarebit) is a classic light meal of grilled cheese with a touch of Worcestershire Sauce, mustard and porter beer often served on toasted bread.

Pembrokeshire Pasty (Pastai Penfro), a tasty pasty made with mutton seasoned with black pepper and mustard.

Pwdin Reis Mam (Mum's Rice Pudding) with sultanas and nutmeg.

Picau ar y Maen (Welsh Cakes), griddle cakes made with spices, currents and sultanas.

TRADITIONAL FOODS OF ENGLAND

Pie, mash and liquor – A classic from the East End of London. It is a cold water pastry pie with a minced beef filling, served with mash potato and 'liquor' – a parsley sauce made from the water that has been used in the preparation of stewed eels.

Jugged Hare – A whole hare, hung for a week or more, jointed, marinated and cooked with red wine and juniper berries in a tall jug stood in a pan of water. This dish is traditionally served with the hare's blood, or the blood is added right at the very end of the cooking process along with some port wine.

Melton Mowbray Pork Pie – Coarse chopped uncured pork and pork jelly sealed in a hand-raised crust. The meat within real Melton Mowbray Pork Pies should appear greyish, not pink.

Norfolk Potted Shrimps – One of the favourites of the late Queen Mother, this dish simply contains cooked shrimps caught in the Wash, potted in butter seasoned with ground mace and cayenne pepper.

Yorkshire Pudding – A batter pudding cooked in the oven in very hot beef dripping, used as an accompaniment for a meal or, if large enough, the meal is served within the pudding.

Toad in the Hole – A variation of Yorkshire Pudding where the batter is poured over some grilled or baked sausages.

Fish and Chips – Battered fish and chipped potatoes, traditionally deep fried in beef dripping, seasoned with salt and vinegar and eaten out of newspaper, lined with a sheet of greaseproof paper. In some parts of Britain the chips are covered in gravy instead of vinegar and mushy peas is considered an essential side order.

Tripe and Onions – Tripe is the stomach lining of an ox, dressed and parboiled with onions and seasoning. This dish is particularly popular in Lancashire and Yorkshire.

Steak and Kidney Pudding – Lean steak and kidney, seasoned and casseroled then poured into a suet pudding case and steamed in boiling water for about two hours.

The English love their suet puddings and enjoy some in sweet forms such as 'Spotted Dick' (the mix contains currants – the so-called 'spots') or Jam Roly Poly.

Bakewell Tart – Shortcrust pastry with a layer of jam and a sponge filling with almonds.

Eton Mess – a mixture of strawberries, pieces of meringue and cream. The dish is believed to have received its name during the nineteenth century when it was first served at the annual cricket game between Eton College and the students of Winchester College.

TRADITIONAL FOODS OF SCOTLAND

Scotch broth – A broth containing lamb, mutton or beef, with pearl barley and root vegetables such as carrots, turnips or swede, leeks or cabbage.

Scotch pie – Small high-sided, double-crust round pastry case with minced lamb or mutton filling with an open top, often sold at football matches and other outdoor sporting events and washed down with a mug of Bovril.

Scotch egg – Hard-boiled egg, cased in sausage meat rolled in breadcrumbs.

Haggis – A savoury pudding made from minced sheep's pluck (heart, liver and lungs), oatmeal, onion, suet, spices and salt mixed with stock; all encased in a sheep's stomach and served after being steamed for about three hours with 'tatties' (potatoes) and 'neeps' (turnips).

Arbroath smokies – Small lightly smoked haddock.

Herrings in oatmeal – Just as the fishermen preferred them.

Scotch Shortbread – Traditionally made from one part white sugar, two parts butter, and three parts flour baked at a low temperature to avoid browning.

Black Bun or Yule Cake – A fine Christmas pudding-like filling surrounded by a delicate envelope of pastry.

Deep fried Mars bar in batter washed down with a glass or two of 'Buckie' (Buckfast Tonic Wine) or Irn-Bru, for that real gourmet touch.

TRADITIONAL FOOD OF NORTHERN IRELAND

Irish Stew – A stew of chunky pieces of lamb, onions and potatoes in beef stock seasoned with black pepper, thyme and parsley.

Baked Ulster Ham – A corner of gammon seasoned with cloves, peppercorns and brown sugar topped with a coating of sugar, cinnamon, whiskey and Guinness. This ham is renowned for its sweetness and succulence

Brown Soda Bread – Wheat flour, white flour, rolled oats, baking soda and salt mixed in a large bowl with buttermilk, then kneaded, moulded into flat loaves, cut with a deep cross to ensure an even rise and baked in the oven. This dish is still made every week in many Irish homes.

Potato Bread – Finely grated potato and mashed potato mixed together with flour, baking soda, buttermilk and occasionally egg, then cooked like a pancake on a griddle pan.

Barmbrack – A yeasted bread with sultanas and raisins.

THE FAVOURITE BRITISH FOOD

Curry is often cited as the most popular food in Britain. It may seem exotic and filled with the spices of India and the Far East but many curries sold in Indian restaurants or as pre-prepared sauces in jars in the UK are those that were tailored for British tastes during the days of the Raj and are nothing like traditional Indian dishes. Restaurants in Great Britain have adopted a number of Indian terms to identify popular dishes. Although the names may be derived from traditional dishes, frequently, the recipes are not. Historically, the word 'curry' was first used in British cuisine back in the eighteenth century, to denote dishes of meat (often leftover lamb) in a Western-style sauce flavoured with curry powder. Madras curry is purely a British invention and vindaloo was brought to India by Britain's oldest ally, the Portuguese, when they first arrived in Goa in the fifteenth century. Furthermore, the phall, renowned and feared for its formidable heat on the palate, is unheard of on the Indian subcontinent and is purely the creation of British Indian restaurants.

HOW DO YOU LIKE THESE APPLES?

There are over 1,200 native British apples for eating and cooking, as well as for cider-making and crab apples for pickling. The oldest apple variety in existence is believed to be the Decio which is thought to date back to the Romans, but the oldest recorded English apple, the Pearmain, was recorded in a Norfolk document of 1204. Here are some more of the old breeds of British apple still to be found in our orchards:

Ashmead's Kernel
Allens Everlasting
Beeley Pippin
Beauty of Bath
Blenheim Orange
Braddick's Nonpareil
Brown's Apple
Catshead
Claygate Pearmain
Cornish Gilliflower
D'Arcy Spice
Devonshire Quarrenden
Duke of Devonshire

Fearn's Pippin
Golden Reinette
Green Balsam
Grimes Golden
Herefordshire Redstreak
Kentish Fillbasket
Pitmaston Pineapple
Ribston Pippin
Royal Somerset
Slops in Wine
Yorkshire Greening (also known
  as the Yorkshire Goosesauce)

MINE'S A PINT OF ...

Some real ale brews with unusual names (with their ABV and breweries):

Old Ma Weasel (3.6%), Ales of Kent
Horny Toad (5%), Tipsy Toad
Last Rites (11%), Abbeydale
Cleric's Cure (5%), Three Tuns
Blandford Fly (5.2%), Badger
Cocklewarmer (4.2%), Swale
Old Peculiar (5.7%), Theakston
Bitter Ol' Bustard (4.3%), Jo C's
Old Knucker (5.5%), Arundel
Whistle Belly Vengeance (4.7%), Summerskills
Trout Tickler (9.9%), Ballard's
Bodmin Beast (5.5%), Sutton
Piddle in the Hole (3.9%), Wyre Piddle
Old Slapper (4.2%), Bank Top
Old Recumbent (5.2%), Six Bells
Highgate Fox's Nob (3.6%), Aston Manor
Dragonslayer (4.5%), B & T
Old Red Eye (4.6%), Brown Cow
Dockyard Rivets (5.1%), Burntisland
Nessie's Monster Mash (4.4%), Cairngorm

Hellfire Jack (4.2%), Boat Brewery
Brodie's Plonker (3.8%), Cannon Royall
Pooh Beer (4.3%), Church End
Dog's Bollocks (5.2%), Wychwood
Rombald's Reviver (3.8%), Briscoe's
Old Black Shuck (4.5%), Elgood's
Cockeyed Goose (5.2%), Goose Eye
Red Hot Poker (4.5%), Berkeley
Noggin's Nog (4.2%), Border
Croak and Stagger (5.6%), Frog Island
Cuddy Luggs (4.2%), Bitter End
Buckswood Dingle (3.6%), Fromes Hill
Pig's Ear (6%), Gribble Inn
Old Tongham Tasty (6%), Hogs Back
Butt Jumper (4.8%), Humpty Dumpty
Goblin Waitress (4.3%), Kitchen
Milk of Amnesia (5.2%), Blue Moon
Piddlebrook (3.8%), Rainbow
Otter of Leith (4.2%), Restalrig
Myrtle's Temper (7%), Barge & Barrel
Luddite (5%), Ryburn
Ronnies Owd Cock (4.0%), Barnsley Beer Company
Brain Dead (7%), Scattor Rock
Bishop's Finger (5%), Shepherd Neame
Talywhacker (5.6%), Leith Hill
Colquhoun's Dark Mischief (5%), Lidstones
Scratching Dog (4.5%), Lloyd's
Rabbie's Ruin (4.6%), Mighty Oak
Nelson's Revenge (4.5%), Woodforde's

JUST POPPING DOWN THE LOCAL . . .

Some curious pub names of the past and present:

Goat & Compasses – Euston Road, Camden
The Gate Hangs Well – Syston, Leicestershire
The Three-Legged Mare – High Petergate, York
Bear and Ragged Staff – Crayford, Kent
Blue Pig – Telford, Shropshire
The Case is Altered – Blo Norton, Norfolk
The Lad in the Lane – Erdington, Birmingham
Crooked Billet – Reading, Berkshire
The Idle Cook – Idle, Bradford, Yorkshire

Bucket of Blood – Phillack, Cornwall
The Winkle – Winklebury, Basingstoke
Printers Devil – Bristol
The Bitter End – Cockermouth, Cumbria
Bettle and Chisel – Delabole, Cornwall
Eagle and Child – Oxford
The Bleeding Wolf – Hale, Altrincham, Cheshire
Butt & Oyster – Pin Mill, Suffolk
The Cow and Snuffers – Llandaff, Cardiff
Tunnel Top – Runcorn, Cheshire
Fox Goes Free – Charlton, West Sussex
See Ho – Shorne, Kent
Oyster Reach – Wherstead, Ipswich
Reckless Engineer – Bristol Temple Meads
Atmospheric Railway – Starcross, Devon
Man Loaded with Mischief – Norwich, Norfolk
Pillar of Salt – Droitwich, Worcestershire
Flying Bedstead – Hucknall, Nottinghamshire
Tappers Harker – Long Eaton, Nottingham
Swan with Two Necks – Pendleton, Clitheroe, Lancashire
Nowhere Inn Particular – Croydon, Surrey
Honest Lawyer – Folkestone
Jolly Taxpayer – Portsmouth
Honest Politician – Portsmouth
Help the Poor Struggler – Manchester Road, Oldham
The Nutshell, Bury St Edmunds, Suffolk (Britain's smallest pub
    measuring just 16.5ft by 6.5ft)

Goat in Boots – Drummond Street, London
Five Miles from Anywhere, No Hurry – Upware, Cambridgeshire
Cock and Bull – Sutton, Surrey
Dirty Dick's – Bishopgate, London
The Blind Beggar – Whitechapel, London
The Old Thirteenth Cheshire Astley Volunteer Rifleman Corps Inn –
   Stalybridge, Greater Manchester (Britain's longest pub name)
The Dirty Habit – Hollingbourne, Kent
I am the Only Running Footman –Mayfair, London
Wait for the Waggon – Wyboston, Bedfordshire
Bull and Mouth – Bloomsbury, London
Humble Plumb – Bitterne, Southampton
Crooked Chimney – Lemsford, Hertfordshire
Hole in the Wall – Little Wilbraham, Cambridgeshire
Man in the Moon – Stanmore, Middlesex
Ye Olde Cheshire Cheese – Fleet Street, London
Olde Man and Scythe – Bolton, Lancashire
Ye Olde Trip to Jerusalem – Nottingham
Slow and Easy – Lostock Gralam, Northwich, Cheshire
Three Goats Head – Oxford
Ye Olde Murenger House – Newport, Monmouthshire
Fatling and Firkin – Hornchurch
Fuzzock and Firkin – Leicester
Sir Loin of Beef – Southsea
The Labour in Vain – Yarnfield, Staffordshire
Lamb and Flag – Oxford
Beartown Tap – Congleton, Cheshire
Shroppie Fly – Audlem, Cheshire
The Spotted Cow – Bloxwich, Walsall, West Midlands
The Pub With No Name – Brighton

8

LEGENDS, GHOSTS & CURIOSITIES

ST GEORGE – THE PATRON SAINT OF ENGLAND

St George is the patron saint of England but little is known for certain about the man himself. He is said to have been a tribune in the Roman Army and was beheaded on the orders of Diolectian for his protests against the emperor's persecution of Christians in the year 303. St George's combat with a dragon is a later symbolic addition to show the conquest by the forces of the good and holy in the form of St George over evil and the devil embodied in the dragon. St George is also the patron saint of soldiers and he is claimed to have appeared before a number of armies over the years including at the Battle of Antioch in 1098 and even the British soldiers at Mons in 1914. The Cross of St George, consisting of the red cross of a martyr on a white background has formed the national flag of England for centuries.

ST ANDREW – THE PATRON SAINT OF SCOTLAND

St Andrew, the brother of St Peter the Apostle, became the patron saint of Scotland in the mid-tenth century when, according to legend, Óengus II led an army of Picts and Scots into battle against the Angles in AD 832. Heavily outnumbered, Óengus prayed and pledged that if he was victorious he would see to it that St Andrew be made patron saint of Scotland. On the morning the clouds formed into the shape of a cross that they interpreted as a sign representing the *crux decussata* upon which the saint had been cruicified. Óengus and his army were victorious in battle and he kept his pledge – the St Andrew's Cross or Saltire, is the national flag of Scotland.

ST PATRICK'S CROSS

Ireland is represented on the British Union flag by the St Patrick's Cross or Saltire added to the Union Flag after the Act of Union in 1800. There is little or no undisputed evidence of the Saltire appearing in Irish heraldry before the creation of the Order of St Patrick created by George III in 1783.

ST DAVID – PATRON SAINT OF WALES

St David was a Welsh bishop in the sixth century recognised as a saint by the Vatican and Pope Callixtus II in 1120. David is said to have lived for over 100 years, and when he died on Tuesday 1 March (now St David's Day) in 589/590 his monastery was said to have been 'filled with angels as Christ received his soul.' His last words to his followers were in a sermon on the previous Sunday, transcribed by Rhygyfarch as 'Be joyful, and keep your faith and your creed. Do the little things that you have seen me do and heard about. I will walk the path that our fathers have trod before us.' His flag (Baner Dewi Sant) consists of a broad yellow cross on a black background.

THE LEEK AS A NATIONAL EMBLEM OF WALES

According to legend, St David ordered his Welsh soldiers to identify themselves by wearing the vegetable on their helmets in an ancient battle against the Saxons that took place in a field of leeks.

KING ARTHUR

The popular British legend of King Arthur has a few ancient roots but its enduring appeal is largely due to the embellished story in Geoffrey of Monmouth's *Historia Regum Britanniae* (*History of the Kings of Britain*), which he completed in 1138. The story was then retold, further embellished and eulogised by Sir Thomas Malory in *Le Morte d'Arthur*, published in 1485. Fact and fiction blend and blur into a wondrous and powerful story of knights and chivalry; of Arthur, his queen, Guinevere; Lancelot and the Knights of the Round Table. Possibly the most enigmatic and mystical of all the tales is *The Noble Tale of the Sangreal – The Quest for the Holy Grail*, the cup used by Christ at the last supper.

The stories of King Arthur and the Holy Grail have become entwined with the myths of the Glastonbury area of Somerset which is identified with the legendary island of Avalon. A local tradition, first recorded by John Leland in 1542, claims that Cadbury Castle was King Arthur's Camelot, some even maintain the grail itself is buried in a secret location in or around Glastonbury. In 1191 the monks at Glastonbury Abbey claimed to have found the graves of Arthur and Guinevere to the south of the Lady Chapel of the Abbey Church.

A number of legends (and locations) across Britain maintain that King Arthur did not die in battle but was wounded and removed to a secret location under a mountain or hill where, with other knights and their trusty mounts, they are but sleeping, held in stasis, only to magically awaken again when Britain is in of dire need of defence.

GLASTONBURY AND THE HOLY GRAIL

One of the most enduring legends of Somerset is that when he was a young boy Jesus had been brought to Somerset by Joseph of Arimathea. After Christ's crucifixion, Joseph returned to Somerset bringing the Holy Grail with him and Glastonbury Abbey was founded at his behest to house it. In this story the grail was not only the cup used at the last supper but was also used by Joseph to catch Jesus's blood at the crucifixion. Joseph is said to have arrived at Glastonbury by boat after crossing the flooded Somerset Levels. On disembarking he stuck his staff into the ground and it flowered miraculously into the Glastonbury Thorn (or Holy Thorn).

ROBIN HOOD

The stories of Robin Hood, the skilled archer and kindly outlaw who, with his merry men, 'robbed the rich and gave to the poor', has a far firmer grounding in fact than many other legends. Although it is difficult to identify the exact man himself, it is clear the tales of Robin Hood are based on those of outlaws in the thirteenth and fourteenth centuries when the names 'Robinhood', 'Robehod', 'Robbehod' or 'Rabunhod' appear in various judicial rolls from regions across England when referring to itinerant criminals. There are clear recorded references to them as far back as the fourteenth century during which the 'rhymes of Robin Hood' are referred to in the poem 'Piers Plowman' by William Langland.

THE LAMBTON WORM

A legendary tale from County Durham where a young knight named John Lambton skips church to go fishing in the River Wear. He catches an eel-like creature with a salamander's head. Lambton is afraid of the creature and, believing he has caught a Devil, he throws it away in a drain or well and shortly afterwards leaves to serve on the Crusades. With time the worm grows and soon villagers begin to notice their livestock are going missing then lo! The fully-grown beast emerges and it is enormous, so big it coils itself around a hill. In some accounts it is Penshaw Hill but the 'favourite' is Worm Hill in Fatfield where it is said the marks of the worm's seven coils around the hill may still be seen.

A number of knights attempt to slay the worm but all are killed in their attempts for as they slice off chunks of the creature it simply reattaches itself. When Lambton returns after a number of years at the Crusades, he finds his father's estate almost ruined because of the worm. He feels the worm and its destructive behaviour are his responsibility and he sees it as his mission and duty to destroy it. He seeks advice on how he could kill the worm from a knowing woman (or in some tales a witch) from Durham. She advises him to affix sharp spearheads to his armour and to fight the worm in the river. This he does and with each cut the piece of the worm is carried away with the flow of the river before it can rejoin the body and thus he slays the beast.

The tragedy comes, however, in the aftermath. The witch told Lambton that he must kill the first living thing he sees once he has slain the worm. He arranges with his father to send his dog on his signal but the old man forgets and rushes out to congratulate his son. Lambton could not bring himself to kill his father and thus a curse was brought upon his family that none of them would die peacefully in their beds for nine generations thereafter.

DRAKE'S DRUM

Shortly before his death, Sir Francis Drake (1540–96) ordered his drum to be taken to his home at Buckland Abbey in Buckland Monachorum, Devon. It remains there to this day, Drake having vowed that if England was ever in danger someone was to beat the drum and he would return to defend the country. It has been claimed that beats and rolls on the drum have been heard when England was at war or significant national events, especially deaths of monarchs, have occurred.

THE BLACK DOG

One of the most ancient and recurrent figures in British myths, legends and folklore is the Black Dog. It is a manifestation that has never been taken lightly; for some it represents a demon of the ancients who no longer receives his supplication and veneration and now lopes along the lanes in the teeth of fierce storms and chime hours to claim souls in retribution. For much of East Anglia the great, shaggy, black devil dog, known by a variety of names such as Old Shuck, Shock, the Shuck Dog and the most popular, Black Shuck, is a terrifying and often malevolent creature associated with storm,

tempest, wrath, vengeance, witchcraft, demons and death. The origin of this name is suggested by some as a derivation of Shuggy or Shaggy, a regional variation of 'scruffy' while others suggest the Anglo-Saxon word, Scucca, meaning devil or demon. In the north of England, in Northumberland, Durham and especially in Yorkshire, accounts can be found of Padfoot and, most notoriously, the Bargest that assumes the form of a large black dog with flaming eyes and is said to frequent a remote gorge named Troller's Gill. There is also a story of a Bargest occasionally entering the city of York, where, according to legend, it preys on lone travellers in the city's narrow Snickelways. On the death of any local worthy in the neighbourhood of Leeds the Bargest was said to come forth, causing all the dogs in the locality to bay and howl. In Lancashire their black dog is known as a Gytrash, Trash or Shriker, while in Wales the black dog is the Gwyllgi, the Dog of Darkness, a frightful apparition of a mastiff with baleful breath and blazing red eyes. The Gurt Dog of Somerset and the Black Dog of Lincolnshire are rare examples of the creature with a benevolent nature. It was said that mothers would allow their children to play unsupervised because they believed that the dog would protect them. It would also be known to accompany lone travellers, acting as a protector and guide.

THE LEGEND OF THE MISTLETOE BOUGH (OR BRIDE)

This tragic tale has become associated with a number of mansions and stately homes in England. The story tells of how a new bride was playing a game of hide-and-seek during her wedding breakfast and hid in a chest in an attic. The hasp closed and locked tight on the outside and the unfortunate bride was unable to escape. Sadly the other players could not work out where she had hidden herself and the poor bride was suffocated. The whole thing remained a mystery and despite continued efforts to find her, her body remained hidden and almost forgotten until it was found many years later when the house was being cleared and the chest, upon being discovered, was forced open.

WANDLEBURY RING

Wandlebury Ring is an Iron Age hill fort in Cambridgeshire that dates back 2,500 years. The legend attached to it, first recorded in *Otia Imperialia* by Gervase of Tilbury in the early twelfth century, tells of how if a knight dared to enter it by moonlight and cried 'Knight to knight, come forth,' a ghostly night-rider would appear and do battle. One such knight was Sir Osbert, who was met by the Black Knight by moonlight. After a fierce exchange, Sir Osbert gained an advantage and knocked the night-rider to the ground. As victor of the contest Osbert claimed his adversary's steed. The infuriated night-rider threw his lance at Osbert and disappeared. The weapon only caught him a glancing cut to the thigh and was quick to heal, but every anniversary of his fight with the night-rider the wound would open up again as if fresh, would bleed profusely and then heal again immediately.

ROLLRIGHT STONES

Witchcraft has been known to have been practiced across Britain for centuries and remains a living belief in the country today. One legend that has been handed down for centuries is that of the Rollright Stones; three Neolithic and Bronze Age megalithic monuments situated near the village of Long Compton on the Oxfordshire and Warwickshire border. The story attached to them is recorded by William Camden in 1586 and tells of a king who was riding through the country when he and his men were accosted by a local witch and turned to stone. The local legend names the witch as Mother Shipton who prophesised unto him:

> Seven long strides shalt thou take, says she
> And if Long Compton thou canst see,
> King of England thou shalt be!

The king's troops gathered in a circle to discuss the challenge and his knights muttered among themselves but the king boldly took seven steps forward. Rising ground blocked his view of Long Compton in the valley and the witch cackled:

> As Long Compton thou canst not see,
> King of England thou shalt not be!
> Rise up stick and stand still stone, For
> King of England thou shalt be none;
> Thou and thy men hoar stones shall be,
> And I myself an elder tree!

The king was turned to stone and became what is now known as 'The King Stone', while his soldiers, also turned to stone and formed a cromlech, or circle nearby called 'The King's Men'. As Mother Shipton prepared to turn herself into an elder tree, she encountered the four muttering king's knights who had lagged behind and were whispering plots against the king. She also turned them to stone and they are now known as 'The Whispering Knights'.

COTTINGLEY FAIRIES

Stories of 'little folk' or fairies can be found down the years across Great Britain but the greatest stir of all occurred when two young girls, cousins Elsie Wright (16) and Frances Griffiths (10) of Cottingley near Bradford, took five photographs of each other with what appeared to be fairies in 1917. No lesser a man than the creator of Sherlock Holmes, Sir Arthur Conan Doyle, saw the photographs as proof of psychic phenomena and used them to illustrate an article he wrote for the Christmas edition of *The Strand Magazine* in 1920. It was a sensation and was revisited again and again over the years until 1983 when Elsie and Francis, by then elderly ladies, admitted that the photographs had been faked . . . but both still maintained that they really had seen fairies.

WAYLAND'S SMITHY

This historic site is actually a Neolithic long barrow near Ashbury in Oxfordshire, but folklore told of how if a horse was left here with suitable payment it would be magically shod while the owner was away and out of sight by the Wayland Smith.

LOCH NESS MONSTER

Modern interest in the Loch Ness 'Monster' was sparked when reports were published in the *Inverness Courier* in August 1933 of a sighting of a strange creature seen crossing the road towards Loch Ness by Mr and Mrs George Spicer. They described the creature as having a large body about 4ft high and 25ft long with a long, narrow neck, slightly thicker than an elephant's trunk with undulations along it. They estimated the neck stretched across the width of the road – 10–12ft. National newspapers picked up the story and it became a sensation fuelled by further sightings followed by the notorious 'Surgeon's Photograph' allegedly showing the Loch Ness Monster, taken by London gynaecologist Robert Kenneth Wilson and published in the *Daily Mail* in April 1934. Hunts and investigations to capture, confirm or disprove the existence of the monster have been staged sporadically ever since but the mystery remains unsolved.

FIGURES IN THE LANDSCAPE

Britain's countryside is filled with wonders and curiosities but probably the most intriguing of them all are hill figures. Only two humanoid figures remain, namely the Long Man of Wilmington marked out on the steep slope of Windover Hill on the South Downs near the village of Wilmington in East Sussex (today he is seen as a 227ft tall outline of a man holding two staffs) and the far more graphic 180ft Cerne Abbas Giant in Dorset. His outline is traced through trenches cut in the hillside grass and depicts a naked man with an apparently erect phallus, a neutral-featured face and a club in his hand. Local legend suggests women wishing to promote their fertility should stand at the head of his member. Although thought to be of earlier, even ancient, origin there is little evidence for either hill figure's existence prior to the seventeenth century. Far more prevalent were White Horses, most of which were also created in the south during the eighteenth and nineteenth centuries. A number of these have also been lost but the most ancient of them all to survive is the

Uffington White Horse in Oxfordshire (historically Berkshire) which dates back over 3,000 years to the Bronze Age.

THUNDER AS HARBINGER

Britain has many sayings and beliefs that chart a vast array of life, luck and portent, but one of the most curious and obscure relates to thunder and was recorded by Leonard Digges in *A Prognostication Everlasting* (1556).

> Sunday's thunder should bring the death of learned men, judges, and others; Monday's thunder the death of women; Tuesday's thunder plenty of grain; Wednesday's thunder the death of harlots; Thursday's thunder plenty of sheep and corn; Friday's thunder, the slaughter of a great man, and other horrible murders; Saturday's thunder a general plague and great dearth.

SOME GREAT BRITISH HAUNTINGS

Britain has a great tradition of haunted houses and places. Here, in no particular order, are ten of the author's favourites:

Blickling Hall, Norfolk – The phantom carriage carrying the headless body of Anne Boleyn, second wife of King Henry VIII, is said to clatter up the driveway at midnight on 19 May, the anniversary of her execution.

Herstmonceux Castle, East Sussex – There are many ghosts in this historic building including a phantom drummer, a grey lady and a woman in white.

Littlecote House, Wiltshire – Home of the infamous 'Wild Will' Darrell in the sixteenth century is haunted by the newborn child he murdered and a number of other spooks.

Postbridge, Devon – A pair of ghostly hairy hands have blighted motorcyclists and car drivers on the road to Two Bridges.

Athelhampton House, Dorset – Has a number of ghosts including the scratching of a ghostly monkey who was accidentally shut away in a secret passage behind the Great Chamber, a grey lady, ghostly duellists, the shadowy figure of a priest or monk in his black robes and the hammering of a long-dead cooper can occasionally be heard in the wine cellar.

The Tower of London – This ancient bastion is haunted by two wives of Henry VIII – Anne Boleyn and Catherine Howard. Lady Jane Grey makes occasional appearances, as does the figure of a long-haired woman wearing a long black velvet dress who appears at a window in the Bloody Tower. Even the ghost of a great bear from the zoo that once existed in the Tower has been reported.

Featherstone Castle, Northumberland – The spectral rattling of chains and agonised moans of Sir Reginald FitzUrse who starved to death in the castle may still be heard. The ghosts of a hideously mutilated bridal party have also been seen on occasion, especially near Pinkeyn Clough where the party were ambushed.

Renishaw Hall, Derbyshire – Haunted by Henry Sacheverell 'The Boy in Pink' who died in 1716, his ghost returns and is felt in one of the bedrooms by three kisses from his cold lips.

Llancaiach Fawr, a Tudor manor house near Nelson, Caerphilly – is said to be haunted by a number of apparitions including a nineteenth-century housekeeper known as 'Mattie', a young boy who fell to his death from one of the upper rooms, the spectre of a man who usually appears to be in deep contemplation and a mysterious figure who wanders the grounds.

Mary King's Close in Edinburgh – is a now underground close in the Old Town area where legend states plague victims were trapped by the local councilmen and left to starve to death in an attempt to stop the spread of the contagion. The unquiet dead are said to still make their presence known here on a regular basis.

9

TRANSPORT

ON THE ROAD

The United Kingdom radial road network totals 29,145 miles of main roads, 2,173 miles of motorways and 213,750 miles of paved roads.

According to the Law Commission, contrary to popular belief, it is not legal for a man to urinate in public, as long it is on the rear wheel of his motor vehicle and his right hand is on the vehicle.

The first person to be convicted of speeding is believed to be Walter Arnold of East Peckham, Kent, who on 28 January 1896 was fined 1*s* plus costs for driving at 8mph.

The Local Government Board stipulated road signs for speed, prohibition and caution in 1904. There were four types of sign:

1. For 10 miles or lower limit of speed – a white ring 18in in diameter with a plate below showing the speed limit in figures.

2. For prohibition – a solid red disc 18in in diameter.

3. For caution (such as dangerous corners, crossroads or precipitous places) – a hollow red equilateral triangle with 18in sides.

4. All other notices under the Act were stipulated to be displayed on diamond-shaped boards.

The Motor Car Act (1903) introduced driving licences, compulsory registration, number plates and raised the 12mph speed limit set in 1896 to 20mph.

The National 'Safety First' Association to promote safety, particularly on the road and in places of work, was formed in 1923.

The first edition of *The Highway Code* was prepared by the Ministry of Transport and published by His Majesty's Stationery Office on 14 April 1931. It sold for one penny.

The lifesaving road reflectors known as 'Cat's Eyes' were invented by Percy Shaw of Boothtown in Halifax in 1933.

The Road Traffic Act (1934) introduced a 30mph limit in built-up areas and compulsory driving tests for all new drivers.

Driving tests were suspended during the Second World War and for one year during the Suez Crisis in 1956.

The driving theory test was introduced in July 1996 as a written examination and updated to a computer-based test in 2000. An additional hazard perception test was introduced in November 2002.

Zebra crossings were introduced to British roads in 1951.

Tufty Fluffytail, an endearing little red squirrel character, was created by Elsie Mills in 1953 to introduce clear and simple safety messages to children such as crossing the road. Tufty's salutary adventures were told in booklets and film animations narrated by Bernard Cribbins. Tufty was joined in his adventures by Harry Hare, Minnie Mole, the naughty Willy Weasel along with Tufty's Mum, Mrs Fluffytail, Mrs Owl the teacher and Policeman Badger, who always popped up in the nick of time to save the children. The popularity of the character led to the creation of The Tufty Club in 1961 and by the early 1970s it had an estimated 2 million members.

The Green Cross Code campaign was created by the National Road Safety Committee (now the Royal Society for the Prevention of Accidents, RoSPA) in 1970.

The costumed superhero character Green Cross Man, created in 1975 as an aid to teaching young children the Green Cross Code, was portrayed on public information films by bodybuilder and competitive weightlifter David Prowse.

In 1976, *Doctor Who* actor Jon Pertwee appeared in a public information film for the Green Cross Code introducing the mnemonic 'SPLINK', which stood for:

> (Find a) Safe (place to cross)
> (Stand on the) Pavement
> Look (for traffic)
> If (traffic is coming, let it pass)
> (When there is) No (traffic near, walk across the road)
> Keep (looking and listening for traffic as you cross).

It was not very successful because most kids could not remember what SPLINK stood for.

In 1974 the *Dad's Army* team featured in two public information films about the use of pelican crossings.

In 1976 a number of public information films promoting the Green Cross Code were made with personalities such as boxer Joe Bugner, footballer Kevin Keegan, Les Gray of the pop group Mud and Alvin Stardust who showed kids how to cross the road safely.

SOME SPARE PARTS ABOUT ICONIC BRITISH CARS

Charles Stewart Rolls and Henry Royce formed Rolls-Royce Limited on 15 March 1906.

The Rolls-Royce Silver Ghost was described as the 'best car in the world' by *Autocar* in 1907.

The chassis and engine of the Rolls-Royce Silver Ghost was used as the basis for a range of Rolls-Royce armoured cars.

The Morgan Plus 8 roadster, produced between 1968 and 2004, had a waiting list (no matter who you were) for most of the years it was in production and once owned was loved by many of the rich and famous, including Brigitte Bardot. Driving a Morgan Plus 8 was an experience claimed to 'make a playboy out of any man.'

The Austin Healey Sprite roadster was announced to the world's press just before the Monaco Grand Prix in Monte Carlo on 20 May 1958. Affectionately known as the 'Frogeye' in Britain, the Sprite was in production from 1958 to 1961.

Bentley Motors Limited was founded by Walter Owen 'W.O.' Bentley on 18 January 1919.

The Morris Minor debuted at the Earls Court Motor Show in London on 20 September 1948.

The Lotus Elise, conceived in early 1994, was first produced in Europe in September 1996 and is capable of speeds up to 150mph. In 2009 a man in Derbyshire was clocked by police driving at 173mph in a 50mph zone but he avoided imprisonment after his defence team claimed his sports car was incapable of travelling that fast.

The Land Rover Mk I launched in 1948 was inspired by the popular Second World War four-wheel drive utility vehicle the Jeep. The choice of colour for the early Land Rovers was dictated by the supplies of military surplus supplies of aircraft cockpit paint so they only came in shades of light green.

The E-Type Jaguar was in production from 1961 to 1975. Designed by the Norfolk-born Loughborough College graduate Malcom Sayer (1916–70), on its release Enzo Ferrari declared the E-Type 'The most beautiful car ever made' and its appeal has endured ever since. In 2008 the E-Type ranked first in the *Daily Telegraph*'s list of the 100 most beautiful cars of all time.

The Triumph Stag was launched in 1970 when it was advertised in *Autocar* as costing £1,995, 17s 6d with soft top only; hard top £2,041 11s 5d or with both for £2,093 15s 10d exclusive of purchase tax. The Stag, produced until 1977, has achieved a cult status and has its own Stag Owner Club.

The Mini was made by the British Motor Corporation (BMC) and its successors from 1959 to 2000. The sportier Mini Cooper S versions were remarkably successful as rally cars, winning the Monte Carlo Rally in 1964, 1965 and 1967.

The Minis used in *The Italian Job* (1969) are all Mark I Austin Mini Cooper S cars. Famous owners of Minis include Peter Sellers, Britt Ekland, Ringo Starr, John Lennon and Marianne Faithfull. A psychedelic version of a Mini owned by George Harrison even appeared in the Beatles movie *Magical Mystery Tour* (1967).

By the time production ceased some 5.3 million Minis had been sold, making it the most popular British car ever made.

The first meeting of the MG Car Club took place at the Roebuck Hotel near Stevenage on 12 October 1930.

One of the most popular pre-war cars produced in Great Britain was the Austin Seven. First produced in 1922, it was affordable and its appeal was reflected in its nickname of the 'Baby Austin'. By the time production finally ended in 1939 some 290,000 cars and vans had been made.

The Aston Martin DB5 was the luxury grand tourer from the DB series named after David Brown, the head of Aston Martin from 1947 to 1972. Produced from 1963 to 1965, only 1,023 of these amazing cars were ever made. The DB5 has obtained a legendary status as the personal car choice of the cinematic incarnations of 007 James Bond. The last Bond DB5 to be sold at auction was one that had been used in both *Goldfinger* and *Thunderball* – retaining some if its film features such as pop-out gun barrels behind the front indicators, a rear-window bullet shield and revolving front number plate, it fetched a cool £2,600,000.

TEN GREAT BRITISH MOTORBIKES

A personal selection by Robin Housego based on his 55 years' experience in the trade and as both a competitive and leisure motorcyclist.

1. The Vincent Black Shadow Series C

2. The Triumph 650cc Trophy 1956

3. Velocette 'Venom' Thruxton

4. BSA Bantam 125/150 Series

5. The A.J.S. 350 Model 16M

6. BSA Goldstar 500cc DBD

7. Scott 500cc (1930s vintage)

8. Brough Superior

9. Norton International Featherbed

10. EMC Split Single

FIVE FACTS ABOUT BRITISH COMMERCIAL FLIGHT

The world's first regular international flight service was provided by the British company Aircraft Transport and Travel who commenced a London to Paris service on 25 August 1919.

Heathrow Airport can trace its history back to 1930 when British aero engineer and aircraft builder Richard Fairey paid the vicar of Harmondsworth £15,000 for a 150-acre plot to build a private airport where he could build and test aircraft. Today, Heathrow Airport deals with the largest volume of international passengers annually in the UK.

British Airways Ltd was formed on 30 September 1935 with the merger of Spartan Air Lines Ltd, United Airways Ltd, United Airlines and Hillman's Airways. The 37 operational aircraft of the combined companies included such aircraft as Armstrong Whitworth Argosy IIs, Spartan Three Seaters, DH.60 Moths, DH.84 Dragons, DH.89 Dragon Rapides, DH.86As and Spartan Cruisers.

The abbreviation BOAC stood for British Overseas Airways Corporation.

From October 2009 to September 2010 UK airports handled a total of 211.4 million passengers.

TEN BRITISH PUBLIC AIRPORTS AND THEIR RUNWAY SURFACES

Beccles Airport (Suffolk) – Concrete/Grass
Clacton Airport (Essex) – Grass
Caernarfon Airport (Wales) – Asphalt
Colonsay Airport (Scotland) – Asphalt
Westray Airport (Orkney) – Gravel
George Best Belfast City Airport (Northern Ireland) – Asphalt
Liverpool John Lennon Airport (England) – Asphalt
London Biggin Hill Airport – Tarmac
Bristol Filton Airport (Gloucestershire) – Concrete
Panshanger Airport (Hertfordshire) – Grass

ON THE BUSES

The first horse-drawn omnibus service in Britain was started by John Greenwood between Pendleton and Manchester in 1824.

An early motor bus service was run in Edinburgh from 1898 to 1901.

The London General Omnibus Company introduced motor buses to the capital in 1902.

Approximately 7,500 red buses carry more than 6 million passengers every weekday in the Greater London area.

There are 19,500 bus stops in London.

In 1950 there were an estimated 16,445 million local bus passenger journeys.

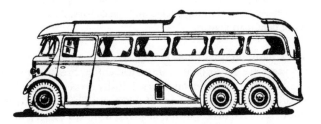

The London transport RT type bus used in the Cliff Richard film *Summer Holiday* (1963) had the fictional number plate of WLB 991.

The pop single 'Magic Bus' by The Who was released in the UK on 18 September 1968.

The TV comedy series *On the Buses* was originally broadcast in six series between 1969 and 1973. The regular cast of characters were:

Stan Butler (Reg Varney)
Bob Grant (Jack Harper)
Mum (Cicely Courtneidge in series 1, Doris Hare in series 2–7)
Olive (Stan's sister, Anna Karen)
Arthur Rudge (Olive's husband, Michael Robbins)
Inspector Cyril 'Blakey' Blake (Stephen Lewis)

Despite looking much older, Stephen Lewis was only in his late thirties when he played 'Blakey' in the TV series.

The exterior shots for the *On the Buses* series were filmed courtesy of the now-defunct Eastern National bus company with buses from their Wood Green bus garage in North London.

LOST PROPERTY

The Transport for London Lost Property Office, tucked by the side of Baker Street station, has been a fixture since 1933 and regularly has around 200,000 items of lost property found on taxis, trains, trams, tubes and stations handed in to it every year.

In 2011 the Lost Property Office received 36,852 books, 28,550 bags and 27,174 items of clothing.

Among the other plentiful items handed in are mobile phones, money, crutches, wheelchairs, walking sticks, umbrellas, toys, false teeth and a variety of dental appliances.

Among the more unusual items commuters have managed to lose in recent years are a 14ft boat, a theatrical coffin, breast implants, power tools, a prosthetic arm, false eyes, full-size dress mannequins, a wedding dress, human skulls, 2.5cwt of sultanas, a Chinese typewriter, a lawnmower, a park bench, a stuffed snake, a stuffed eagle, a divan bed, water skis, a Bishop's crozier, an inflatable doll, a grandfather clock, a Tibetan bell, a jar of bull's semen, a vasectomy kit, a harpoon gun and two urns of ashes.

REGIONS OF THE SHIPPING FORECAST AND WHO OR WHAT THEY WERE NAMED AFTER

Viking – An area covering the open sea between Norway and the Shetland Islands.

North Utsire and South Utsire – Utsire (or Utsira) is a tiny island of 4 square miles off the west coast of Norway populated by about 240 people.

Forties – An area in the North Sea named after a sandbank and an area called the 'Long Forties' that is fairly consistently 40 fathoms deep.

Cromarty – Both a river estuary and a place, Cromarty, in the Burgh of Ross and Cromarty on the north-eastern tip of Scotland.

Forth – The river estuary of the Firth of Forth.

Tyne – The river estuary of the River Tyne.

Dogger – A North Sea sandbank about 160 miles long and 60 miles wide.

Fisher – A sandbank off the west coast of Denmark.

German Bight (formerly Heligoland) – An area between the two headlands of the Netherlands and Denmark.

Humber – The area around the estuary of the River Humber on the east coast of northern England.

Thames – The estuary of the River Thames.

Dover – The town and the Dover Strait, the narrowest part of the English Channel.

Wight – The Isle of Wight.

Portland – An area 5 miles south of Weymouth.

Plymouth – The city of Plymouth on the coast of Devon.

Biscay – The Bay of Biscay, an area to the west of France, forming a gulf of the north-east Atlantic Ocean.

Trafalgar – The headland Cape Trafalgar in Southern Spain.

FitzRoy – Formerly Finisterre, it was renamed in 2002 to honour the distinguished meteorologist Robert FitzRoy, the man who created the Shipping Forecast.

Sole – The Great and Little Sole Banks, sandbanks to the west of the Isles of Scilly in the Atlantic Ocean.

Lundy – An island in the Bristol Channel.

Fastnet – The Fastnet rock is a rock island 6.5 miles to the south-west of Cape Clear in south-west Ireland.

Irish Sea – The Irish Sea is situated between England and Ireland from St David's Head to the Mull of Galloway.

Shannon – The river estuary of the Shannon.

Rockall – An islet or rock stack in the North Atlantic, thought to be the eroded core of an extinct volcano.

Malin – Malin Head on the Inishowen Peninsula; the most northerly headland on the mainland of Ireland.

Hebrides – The area around the islands of the Hebrides, off the north-west coast of Scotland.

Bailey – A sandbank in the North Atlantic between Scotland and Ireland.

Fair Isle – The area around the island of Fair Isle between Orkney and Shetland.

Faeroes – The string of craggy Faeroe (or Faroe) Islands between Scotland and Iceland.

South-East Iceland – An area of the Atlantic south-east of Iceland.

10

NATURAL HISTORY

SOME OF THE FOSSIL TYPES TO BE FOUND IN GREAT BRITAIN

Bivalves
Gastropods
Echinoids
Belemnites
Ammonites
Brachiopods
Shark teeth
Starfish
Sponges
Trilobites
Crinoids
Coprolite (fossilised dinosaur poo)

THE INDIGENOUS EVEN-TOED UNGULATES OF GREAT BRITAIN

Most ungulates use the tips of their toes, usually hoofed, to sustain their whole body weight while moving. The weight of even-toed ungulates is borne about equally by the third and fourth toes.

Wild Boar *Sus scrofa* (reintroduced)
Feral goat *Capra aegagrus hircus* – Bilberry goat

Sheep *Ovis orientalis aries* – Soay sheep
Cattle *Bos primigenius taurus* – Chillingham wild cattle
Scottish red deer *Cervus elaphus scoticus*
Moose *Alces alces alces* (reintroduced)
Roe Deer *Capreolus capreolus*
Reindeer *Rangifer tarandus* (reintroduced)
Elk *Cervus canadensis* (reintroduced)

GREAT BRITISH TITS – A SPOTTER'S GUIDE

Great Britain has many varieties of tits that brighten our hedgerows, parks and gardens. The varieties of these gregarious little birds commonly found in Great Britain are:

The Blue Tit (*Cyanistes caeruleus*): Distinctive for its azure blue, yellow and green plumage, it is one of Britain's most recognisable garden visitors.

Bearded Tit (*Panurus biarmicus*): A long-tailed bird with brown plumage found only in reedbeds.

The Great Tit (*Parus major*): The largest of the tit family, it is also distinguished by its bluish-black crown, black neck, throat, bib and head, a fine bright yellow breast, white cheeks and ear coverts.

The Long-Tailed Tit (*Aegithalos caudatus*): Recognisable for its tail that is longer than its body. This tit is commonly found in woodland, hedgerows and suitable bushes on heath, common, park or garden.

The Coal Tit (*Periparus ater*): Has a plumage that consists of a distinctive grey back, a black cap, and white patch at the back of its neck. These little rascals are regular visitors to garden peanut feeders and smuggle the food away to eat later.

The Crested Tit (*Lophophanes cristatus*): Not quite as colourful as most other tits it is more distinctive than all the others because of its upstanding black and white crest and 'bridled' face pattern. Crested Tits are predominantly found foraging up the trunk and along the branches of the trees in Caledonian pine forests.

The Marsh Tit (*Poecile palustris*): A small tit with a mostly brown plumage, shiny black cap, dark 'bib' and pale breast. Very similar in appearance to the Willow Tit, ornithologists did not realise they were two separate species until 1897. Despite what their name might imply, Marsh Tits are most at home in broadleaf woodland, copses, parks and gardens.

The Willow Tit (*Poecile montanus*): Very similar in appearance to the Marsh Tit, their plumage has subtle differences, most obvious of all that its wings show a pale panel that is not found in Marsh Tits. Willow Tits tend to inhabit willow thickets in damp places.

TEN RANDOM FACTS ABOUT BRITISH NATURAL HISTORY

There are 25 species of bumblebee in the United Kingdom.

There are more than 1,800 species of lichen in the British Isles and 600 species of moss in the UK.

There are currently 25 species of seabird that breed in Britain and Ireland.

The most abundant seabird in Britain and Ireland is the Common Guillemot, of which there are an estimated 1.6 million.

Adders are the only venomous snakes in the United Kingdom.

Bewick's swans are the smallest and rarest of the three species of swan found in the British Isles.

The Fen Raft spider, the adult of which has a legspan of 4 inches across, is the largest spider native to the UK. It is not surprising that it is also one of the country's most endangered species of spider.

Britain's largest freshwater fish of modern times was a monster carp, nicknamed Two Tone, who weighed almost 68lbs and was believed to have been about 45 years old when found floating dead (from old age) at Conningbrook Lake at Mid Kent Fisheries in Chilham, near Canterbury in 2010.

Britain's largest deer was a 12-year-old 9ft red deer stag known as The Emperor of Exmoor, master of the largest deer herd in England, said to be some 3,000 strong. Emperor, estimated to have weighed a massive 300lbs, was reported as being shot by hunters in a field on the edge of Exmoor near Rackenford, Devon, in October 2010.

The Roman Snail, known in culinary circles as *Escargot,* is Britain's largest snail and can live for up to 20 years. Found only in western and southern England, it has become rare through over-hunting and poaching and as a result has been designated in England as a protected species under the Wildlife and Countryside Act 1981, making it illegal to kill, injure, collect or sell them.

ATTACK OF THE MYSTERY SPIDERS!

A colony of unidentified spiders with leg spans of up to 9cm, claimed to be venomous and able to bite through skin, were said to have been discovered by British Telecom engineers who fled in fear from the utility tunnels under Windsor Castle where they found them in June 2001. Once photos of the spiders were published arachnologists rapidly identified them as *Meta menardi,* a common and inoffensive spider, with half the leg span published in the initial media hype, common to dark caves and tunnels in Britain and Europe.

TREE TALK

Many ancient yew trees in British churchyards pre-date the churches they stand near and are believed, in many instances, to mark pagan burial grounds.

The Fortingall Yew in the churchyard of the village of Fortingall in Perthshire is estimated to be well in excess of 2,000 years old. Other yews that claim similar vintage may be found at Discoed in Powys and Llangernyw in Conwy.

The Ankerwyke Yew in Berkshire is also believed to be about 2,000 years old.

An oak tree can live for 1,000 years or more.

Britain's tallest tree is believed to be a 211ft grand fir planted in the 1870s beside Loch Fyne in Argyll.

A sessile oak growing in the grounds of Croft Castle, Herefordshire, stands a whopping 115ft tall and has a trunk that is 9ft thick at its base. With a volume calculated at 3,800 cu ft, it is believed to be Britain's biggest living thing.

Folklore holds that carrying any piece of oak draws good luck to you and if you catch a falling oak leaf you shall have no colds all winter.

A number of maritime heroes such as Nelson and Collingwood would carry acorns in their pocket and give them as gifts so that they may be planted to grow more trees to maintain the supply of wood for our ships of the line.

The horse chestnut tree, beloved for its conkers, and believed to be so quintessentially British is, in fact, a native of the Balkans.

One of the rarest of all British trees is known as the Audley End oak (*Quercus audleyensis*), planted in 1772 in the grounds of the magnificent estate at Audley End, Essex. A number of attempts have been made to plant grafts from the tree but all, so far, have perished.

RABBIT, RABBIT

Many people do not realise that rabbits, which are such a common feature of the British countryside today, are not an indigenous species to our islands. Native to the dry and sandy soil of the Mediterranean region they were, in fact, introduced by the Normans. In those times rabbits were highly prized luxuries, popular at feasts and their fur used to line or trim the clothing of the well-to-do. To give some idea to their value, in the thirteenth century a rabbit cost more than a skilled craftsman earned in a day. Rabbit warrens were the preserve of the most wealthy and powerful in medieval England – the titled gentry and monastic institutions, who had the land and could afford to maintain them. Warrens varied in size from about a furlong to some instances where they would stretch over 1,000 acres.

NON-NATIVE ANIMALS TO BE FOUND IN THE BRITISH COUNTRYSIDE

Red Necked Wallaby from Australia
American Mink
Canada Geese
Coypu from South America (subsequently eradicated)
Chinese Water Deer
Common Pheasant
Golden Pheasant
Grey Squirrel
Rabbit from Mediterranean Europe
Rose-ringed Parakeet from Asia
Sika Deer from Asia

FIFTEEN ANIMALS AND BIRDS NOW EXTINCT IN BRITAIN

Aurochs – An ancient ancestor of modern cattle (extinct since *c.* 1000 BC).

Beech or Stone marten – An attractive member of the mammalian family of martens still to be found in some parts of Europe (nineteenth century).

Brown Bear (*c.* AD 1000).

Eurasian Cave Lion (*c.* 10,000 BC)

Great Auk – A flightless bird hunted for centuries for its meat, eggs and feathers. The last Great Auk seen in the British Isles was caught and killed on the islet of Stac an Armin, St Kilda, in July 1840. It is now completely extinct (AD 1840).

Great Bustard – Once a popular bird for its easy hunting and tasty meat, it has been extinct in Britain for about 180 years although attempts are now being made to reintroduce the bird.

Great White Pelican (*c.* 1,000 BC).

Grey Wolf (*c.* AD 1680).

Irish Elk (*c.* 6,000 BC).

Narrow-headed vole (*c.* 8,000 BC).

Pika – A small mammal, a distant relative of rabbits and hares, with short limbs, rounded ears and no external tail (*c.* 8,000 BC).

Saiga Antelope (*c.* 10,000 BC).

Tarpan (*c.* 7,000 BC) – A subspecies of wild horse, now completely extinct.

Walrus (1,000 BC).

Woolly Mammoth (*c.* 10,000 BC).

BUTTERFLIES

There are 59 species of butterfly that breed in Britain. In the summertime our gardens may be graced with the likes of Chalkhill

Blue, Red Admiral, Small Tortoiseshell, Scotch Argus, Large White, Common Blue, Grayling and Gatekeeper, but there are also rare breeds that can be occasionally seen if we are lucky enough to spot them. Here are ten rare butterflies, most of them migrants, occasionally to be seen in Britain:

Apollo (*Parnassius apollo*)
American Painted Lady (*Cynthia virginiensis*)
Berger's Clouded Yellow (*Colias alfacariensis*)
Camberwell Beauty (*Nymphalis antiopa*)
Dappled White (*Euchloe crameri*)
Long-tailed Blue (*Lampides boeticus*)
Monarch (*Danaus plexippus*)
Pale Clouded Yellow (*Colias hyale*)
Queen of Spain Fritillary (*Issoria lathonia*)
Swallowtail – Britain's largest native butterfly and one of the rarest.

HEDGEHOG

One of the animals that epitomises the British countryside is the hedgehog, the only British mammal with spines. The name is believed to have become common parlance in about 1450 and is derived from the Middle English *heyghoge*, from *heyg*, *hegge* ('hedge'), because it frequents hedgerows, and *hoge*, *hogge* ('hog'), from its pig-like snout and grunt. Country cures obtained from gypsies were considered particularly potent and a number of these were based around hedgehogs as the principal ingredient. Gypsies were known for eating our spiny friends after baking them in mud casings . . . when the mud was peeled away, the spines went with it leaving just the cooked meat. New mothers were often prescribed this food as it was believed to enrich their blood after childbirth, while it was also offered as a treatment for those suffering with anaemia, rheumatism or arthritis.

TYPES OF DOLPHIN FOUND IN WATERS AROUND THE BRITISH ISLES

Short-beaked Common Dolphin (*Delphinus delphis*)
Bottlenose Dolphin (*Tursicops truncatus*)
Striped Dolphin (*Stenella coeruleeoalba*)
Atlantic White-sided Dolphin (*Lagenorhynchus acutus*)
White-beaked Dolphin (*Lagenorhynchus albirostris*)
Risso's Dolphin (*Grampus griseus*)

11

SPORTS ROUNDUP

FOOTBALL

A report on one of the earliest recorded football matches in London was penned by William FitzStephen sometime between 1174 and 1183 when he wrote a description of the activities of London youths during the annual festival of Shrove Tuesday:

> After lunch all of the city's youth would go out into the fields to take part in a ball game. The students of each school have their own ball; the workers from each city craft are also carrying their balls. Older citizens, fathers, and the wealthy would come on horseback to watch their juniors competing, and to relive their own youth vicariously: you can see their inner passions aroused as they watch the action and get caught up in the fun being had by the carefree adolescents.

In another early account of a ball-kicking game, which was held in 1280 at Ulkham, near Ashington in Northumberland, a player died after running against an opposing player's dagger.

The first attempt to set out some formal rules for the game of football were the Cambridge Rules, created in 1848.

The 1863 rules of the Football Association provide the first reference in the English Language to the verb to 'pass' a ball.

The first international football match was played on 5 March 1870 between representatives of England and Scotland at The Oval, London.

The first FA Cup final was contested in 1872. The winners of the match, held at The Kennington Oval, were the Wanderers, who beat Royal Engineers 1–0.

The current FA Cup trophy has been in use since 1911.

The Football League was created in 1888 by Aston Villa director William McGregor.

Founded in 1886, and originally based in Woolwich, Arsenal was London's first professional football club and the first London team to become English League Champions, in 1931.

The football net was invented by Liverpool civil engineer John Alexander Brodie in 1891.

The first football cup for women came into existence during the First World War and was popularly known as the Munitionettes' Cup. Competed for by female munitions workers' teams in north-east England, it was officially titled the Tyne Wear & Tees Alfred Wood Munition Girls Cup. The first winners of the trophy were Blyth Spartans.

CRICKET

Cricket is an old sport but exactly where and when it began is unclear. The earliest recorded mention of the game found to date appears in a court case from 1598 over a dispute that arose for ownership of some common land in Guildford, Surrey, during which John Derrick testified that he and his school friends had played *creckett* on the site fifty years earlier when they attended the Free School.

The Laws of Cricket were codified for the first time in 1744.

British soldiers played a cricket at Bois de la Cambre Park in Brussels on 17 June 1815 – the eve of the Battle of Waterloo. The park area where that match took place has been known as La Pelouse des Anglais (the Englishmen's lawn) ever since.

William Gilbert Grace, better known as 'W.G.', made his first-class debut in 1865. Grace became the first batsman to score a century before lunch in a first-class match when he made 134 for Gentlemen of the South v Players of the South at The Oval in 1873. In the same season, he became the first player ever to complete the 'double' of 1,000 runs and 100 wickets in a season, a feat he would achieve on a further eight occasions. Grace played his last match in August 1914 and died just over a year later on 23 October 1915.

Our Village Bowling

The Draper bowls slow

Young Jarge is fast

The Chauffeur thinks he can bowl

The Publican knows
he can't bowl

The Curate would
love to bowl

The Chemist has never
been asked to bowl

Giles has no
wish to bowl

The Squire expects
to bowl

But it's Adam Goldhart
that gets the wickets

The highest-ever recorded score in cricket was achieved by A.E.J. Collins with 628 runs not out in June 1899.

In 1889 the four-ball over was replaced by a five-ball over. This was changed to the current six balls per over in 1900.

RUGBY

Games where participants attempt to run with a ball to a delineated area of the opposing team have been around in Britain for centuries, but the beginning of the modern game of Rugby begins with a legend. The story is that of Rugby schoolboy William Webb Ellis who, showing fine disregard for the rules of football, picked up a ball and ran with it. It originates from Matthew Bloxam, a local antiquarian and former pupil of Rugby School, who published the story in the school magazine *The Meteor* in October 1876. In another letter to the magazine in December 1880, Bloxham elaborated:

A boy of the name Ellis – William Webb Ellis – a town boy and a foundationer . . . whilst playing Bigside at football in that half-year [1823], caught the ball in his arms. This being so, according to the then rules, he ought to have retired back as far as he pleased, without parting with the ball, for the combatants on the opposite side could only advance to the spot where he had caught the ball, and were unable to rush forward till he had either punted it or had placed it for someone else to kick, for it was by means of these placed kicks that most of the goals were in those days kicked, but the moment the ball touched the ground the opposite side might rush on. Ellis, for the first time, disregarded this rule, and on catching the ball, instead of retiring backwards, rushed forwards with the ball in his hands towards the opposite goal, with what result as to the game I know not, neither do I know how this infringement of a well-known rule was followed up, or when it became, as it is now, a standing rule.

The claim was first investigated by the Old Rugbeian Society in 1895 and sadly no first-hand evidence to substantiate the story was forthcoming. Despite the lack of proof, the tale still provides a fine folkloric beginning for the modern game of Rugby.

SPORTS SELECTION

On 25 August 1875 Matthew Webb became the first person to swim the English Channel. He started from Admiralty Pier in Dover and made the crossing to Calais in 21 hours and 45 minutes.

Among the early pioneers of modern British Field Hockey were Teddington Cricket Club in 1871. They wanted a winter activity and experimented with a 'stick' game, based loosely on the rules of Association Football, which they played on the smooth outfield of their cricket pitch using a cricket ball.

The Great Britain Team won the Ice Hockey European Championship 1910 – the first ice hockey tournament for European countries associated to the International Ice Hockey Federation.

The British Open Golf Championship is the oldest of all the Majors and was first held at the Prestwick Golf Club in 1860.

Henry VIII enjoyed a game of tennis so much that he had courts built at Hampton Court and at a number of his other royal palaces.

The All England Lawn Tennis and Croquet Club was originally founded as the All England Croquet Club in 1868 with grounds off Worple Road, Wimbledon. Lawn tennis was just an aside and originally there was only one lawn set apart for the purpose of playing the game. The first tennis championships in men's singles were held to raise money for a pony-drawn roller for the club's croquet lawns in 1877, when the club changed its name to the All England Croquet and Lawn Tennis Club.

The game of rackets, an early forerunner of squash, was created in the early eighteenth century by prisoners at the Fleet debtors' prison in London.

Francis Chichester was the first person to achieve a true single-handed circumnavigation of the world from west to east via the great capes. Sailing his yawl *Gipsy Moth IV* out of Plymouth on 27 August 1966, he returned there on 28 May 1967 having achieved the feat after 226 days of sailing.

The English Amateur Billiards Championship is one of the world's oldest sporting championships. It dates back to 1888 when the first contest ended with H.A.O. Lonsdale defeating W.D. Courtney 500–334 for the title.

The sport of curling has been played in Scotland for over 500 years.

The first world championship for curling, known as the Scotch Cup, was held in Falkirk and Edinburgh in 1959.

Britain's most successful orienteer is Yvette Baker.

The Badminton Horse Trials were first held in 1949 and were advertised as 'the most important horse event in Britain'. The first Badminton had 22 horses from Britain and Ireland and was won by Golden Willow.

The oldest bowls green still played on is in Southampton, where records show that the green has been in operation since 1299.

The first Inter-County Crown Green bowls matches took place in 1893 when Yorkshire and the combined counties of Lancashire & Cheshire began playing friendly matches.

The first medieval Archery Law was passed in 1252 when all Englishmen between the ages of 15 and 60 years were ordered to equip themselves with a bow and arrows.

Edward III banned the game of football in June 1349. His reasons were simple – football and other recreations distracted the populace from practicing archery, which was a necessary skill for Englishmen in the event of war.

The Archery Law of 1363 made it obligatory for all Englishmen between 7 and 60 years of age to practise their skills with the longbow for at least two hours on Sundays and festival days on pain of death.

The oldest continually held race has been staged at Carnwath in Scotland since 1508 and still maintains the same prize for the winner – a pair of hand-knitted knee-length hose.

The longest recorded boxing match was fought over 276 rounds in a contest that lasted 4 hours 30 minutes before Jack Jones secured victory over Pat Tunney in Cheshire in 1825.

The longest recorded bareknuckle fight dragged on 186 rounds over 6 hours and 3 minutes between Bill Hayes and Mike Madden at Edenbridge, Kent, in 1849. Hayes was the eventual victor.

Carpenter Brian Gamlin from Bury invented a dartboard numbering layout in 1896 that is still used on all standard matchplay dartboards to this day.

Darts first appeared on British television in 1962 when Westward Television broadcast the Westward TV Invitational to the south-west of England.

The world record for the most bullseyes scored in ten hours was 1,505, scored by Jon Watson, Bill Foot, Matty Wilson, Del Fox, Gary Ellis, Bryan Pidgeon, Sean Kerry and Bob Anderson at the Winnersh British Legion Club in Winnersh, Wokingham, Berkshire, on 9 January 2011.

The first time the modern Olympic Games were staged in Britain was at the specially built White City Stadium in London from 27 April to 31 October 1908. It had been planned to stage this Olympiad in Italy but they had to pull out after the eruption of Vesuvius. At this Olympics Britain won an amazing 56 gold medals.

Joe Davis was the World Professional Snooker Champion on an unsurpassed 15 occasions between 1927 and 1946.

Reg Park was the first British winner of the title 'Mr Universe', in 1951.

The first Greyhound Grand National was held at the White City Stadium, London, in 1927 and was won by Entry Badge.

The World Pooh Sticks Championships are staged annually on the last Sunday in March at Little Wittenham, Oxfordshire.

Jayne Torvill and Christopher Dean became the highest scoring figure skaters of all time (for a single programme) at the 1984 Winter Olympics where the pair received twelve perfect 6.0s and six 5.9s which included artistic impression scores of 6.0 from every judge.

The first World Conker Championships were staged at Ashton, Northamptonshire, in 1965.

The World Toe Wrestling Championship is held annually on a Saturday early in June in Fenny Bentley, Derbyshire.

Britain's greatest living bowls player is David Bryant (b. 1931), winner of the World (outdoors) singles bowls championship in 1966, 1980 and 1988 and three-time World indoors singles champion (in 1979, 1980 and 1981). He also won the Commonwealth Games singles bowls championship in 1962, 1970, 1974 and 1978.

The winner of the first International Cross-Country Championship, held at Hamilton Park Race Course in Glasgow in 1903, was Albert Shrubb of England.

The Tour of Britain cycling race, otherwise known as the 'Milk Race', was first held in 1951 and was won by Ian Steel of the Vikings.

Croquet is descended from a game introduced to Britain from France during the reign of Charles II. It was played under the name of paille-maille or pall mall, derived from Latin words for ball and mallet.

In 1930 Marjorie Foster became the first woman to win the King's Prize at the National Rifle Championships at Bisley.

The United All-England Croquet Association was founded in Roehampton by Walter Peel and Captain Drummond in 1897.

The Willis setting of six hoops and one peg for croquet was introduced in England in 1922 and remains the most used layout to the present day.

The Paralympic Games originated as the Stoke Mandeville Games, which were first held at Stoke Mandeville Hospital in Buckinghamshire in 1948.

SPEED KINGS

The Formula One World Drivers' Championship is awarded by the Fédération Internationale de l'Automobile (FIA) to the most successful Formula One racing car driver over a season determined by a points system based on Grand Prix results. It has been won by the following Great British drivers:

1962	Graham Hill	BRM
1963	Jim Clark	Lotus
1964	John Surtees	Ferrari
1965	Jim Clark	Lotus
1968	Graham Hill	Lotus

1969	Jackie Stewart	Matra
1971	Jackie Stewart	Tyrrell
1973	Jackie Stewart	Tyrell
1976	James Hunt	McLaren
1992	Nigel Mansell	Williams
1996	Damon Hill	Williams
2008	Lewis Hamilton	McLaren
2009	Jenson Button	Brawn GP

HORSE RACING – THE CLASSICS

The five English Classics are all for three-year-old horses. These races are:

1,000 Guineas – Run at Newmarket over 1 mile (first run in 1814)
2,000 Guineas – Run at Newmarket over 1 mile (first run in 1809)
The Derby – Run at Epsom over 1½ miles (first run in 1780)
The Oaks – Run at Epsom over 1½ miles (first run in 1779)
St Leger – Run at Doncaster over 1 mile 6 furlongs and 132 yards
    (first run in 1776)

SOME GREAT BRITISH WIMBLEDON SINGLES CHAMPIONS

Men's Singles
The Revd John Hartley (1879–80)
William Remshaw (1881–6 and 1889)
Wilfred Baddeley (1891–2 and 1895)
Reginald Doherty (1897–1900)
Laurence Doherty (1902–6)
Arthur W. Gore (1901 and 1908–9)
Fred Perry (1934–6)

Women's Singles

Maud Watson (1884–5)

Lottie Dod (1887–8 and 1891–3)

Charlotte Cooper (1895–6, 1898 and 1901 under her married name of Charlotte Sterry)

Blanche Hillyard (1897, 1899–1900)

Dorothea Douglass (1903–4, 1906 and 1910–11, 1913–14 under her married name of Dorothea Lambert Chambers)

FIFTEEN TYPICALLY BRITISH SPORTS COMMENTATORS

John Arlott (1914–91), journalist and commentator for BBC's *Test Match Special* 1957–80.

Brian 'Johnners' Johnston (1912–94), BBC cricket commentator and presenter from 1946 until his death in 1996.

Henry 'Blowers' Blofeld (b. 1939), first class cricketer 1958–60, joined the *Test Match Special* team in 1972.

Murray Walker (b. 1923), commissioned into the Royal Scots Greys, he commanded a Sherman tank during the Battle of the Reichswald with the 4th Armoured Brigade in 1945. Walker made his first broadcast for the BBC at Shelsley Walsh hillclimb in 1948 but became best known as an F1 motorsport commentator from 1978.

Henry Longhurst (1909–78), BBC commentator 'the voice of golf' from the late 1950s and into the 1970s.

Peter Alliss (b. 1931), a professional golfer between 1947 and 1975, he won 23 tournaments and even gave Sean Connery golf tips before the filming of *Goldfinger*. His popularity as a golf commentator has even seen him present over 140 *Pro Celebrity Golf* television programmes and his own golf show *A Round with Alliss*.

Ted Lowe (1920–2011), known for his hushed tones on the lip microphone, Lowe was the unmistakable voice of BBC television snooker coverage and the popular television snooker tournament *Pot Black* from 1969.

Jimmy Hill (b. 1928), played for Brentford and Fulham, he managed Coventry and has been reporting and presenting television football coverage since 1968.

David Coleman (b. 1926), worked as a sports commentator for the BBC for almost fifty years. Coleman was also the presenter of the long-running BBC sports quiz programme *A Question of Sport*. He will, however, be best remembered for his frequent inane comments – *Private Eye* magazine even named its sports bloopers column 'Colemanballs' in recognition of David's unique talent.

Kenneth Wolstenholme (1920–2002), a bomber pilot with the RAF from 1941, Wolstenholme flew 100 missions over Germany and was awarded the DFC and bar. He was a BBC sports commentator in the 1950s and '60s but will forever be remembered for his commentary during the 1966 World Cup final, which included the now-immortal words, 'some people are on the pitch . . . they think it's all over . . . it is now!' as Geoff Hurst scored England's fourth goal.

John Motson (b. 1945), began as a sports presenter on BBC Radio 2 and replaced Kenneth Wolstenholme on *Match of the Day*. In 2001 a football fan survey voted Motson as 'the perfect voice for football commentary'.

Len Martin (1919–95), born in Australia, Len came on holiday to Britain in 1953 and never went back. He was the voice of the football results on the BBC Saturday afternoon sports programme *Grandstand* from the first edition of the programme in 1958 until his death in 1995.

Harry Carpenter (1925–2010), starting out as a sporting journalist for several national newspapers, Carpenter joined the BBC in 1949 and was their regular boxing correspondent from 1962 until 1994.

John Oaksey (1929–2012), aristocrat John Geoffrey Tristram Lawrence, 4th Baron Trevethin, 2nd Baron Oaksey, has been a familiar racing commentator since he joined ITV in 1969.

Des Lynam (b. 1942), born in Ireland he moved with his family Brighton when he was six. His laid-back style and unique wit made him an immensely popular commentator since he first appeared on Sportswide, part of the current affairs magazine programme *Nationwide* in 1977.

12

SENSE OF PLACE – QUINTESSENTIALLY BRITISH

FAIRS AND FESTIVALS

Britain is an ancient country and has many quirky and unusual local events, several of which have ancient and obscure origins. Some have been lost, while others are comparatively new but have become well-loved and established in their communities. What follows is a brief calendar of some Great British occasions past and present.

January
Mapleton Bridge Jump, Okeover Bridge, Mapleton, Derbyshire (New Year's Day).

Ponteland Wheelbarrow Race, Northumberland (New Year's Day).

Twelfth Day Eve (5 January). English rustic festival to secure a blessing for the fruits of the earth.

Haxey Hood, North Lincolnshire (6 January). A scrimmage of men push the hood to one of four pubs where it remains on display until the following year.

Plough Monday, the first Monday after the twelfth day of Christmas. The traditional beginning of the English Agricultural Year.

Whittlesea Straw Bear Festival, Cambridgeshire. A man dresses entirely in straw and dances about the village in return for gifts.

The Burning of the Clavie, Burghead, Morayshire (11 January).
A bonfire of casks.

Hen Galan, Llandysul, Pembrokeshire (13 January). Singing in the
new year, as per the Julian calendar.

Carhampton Wassailing, Somerset (17 January). A ritual enacted to
ensure a good apple harvest.

The Feast of St Agnes (Eve 20 and Day 21 January). A holiday for
women.

Burns Night (25 January). A celebration of Robert Burns across
Scotland and at gatherings held by Caledonians and sympathisers
across Britain and beyond.

Up Helly Aa (last Tuesday in January). A viking fire festival held in
Lerwick, Shetland.

February
Cradle-Rocking Ceremony, Blidworth, Nottinghamshire (the Sunday
following 2 February).

St Ives Hurling, Cornwall (first Monday after 3 February).

Jethart Hand Ba, Jedburgh, Roxburgh (Borders). A kind of mass medieval football game.

Lynn Mart, Norfolk (14 February). The traditional start of the English Fair circuit.

Shrovetide Football, Alnwick, Northumberland; Sedgefield, Durham and Ashbourne, Derbyshire.

Shrove Tuesday Pancake Races – held across England.

March
Whuppity Stourie, Lanark, Strathclyde (1 March).

Dorking Wife-Carrying Races, Surrey. A self-explanatory event.

Hare Pie Scramble, Hallaton, Leicestershire. A local custom which begins with a church service and rapidly descends into a kind of riot.

Washing Molly Grime. In the church of Glentham, Lincolnshire, a tomb with a figure, popularly called Molly Grime, was washed every Good Friday by seven old maids of the village with water brought from Newell Well, each receiving a shilling for her trouble, in consequence of an old bequest connected with some property in that district. The custom was discontinued in about 1832, when the property was sold without any reservation of the rent-charge for this bequest.

Pace Egg Rolling – Preston, Lancashire and Scarborough, North Yorkshire. Basically rolling eggs down hills.

Whitby Gothic Weekend, North Yorkshire (a late weekend in March or April).

April
All Fools' Day (1 April). Jokes, japes and tricks played across Britain.

Palm Sunday Gad Whip Service, Caistor, Lincolnshire.
A representative of the proprietor of the Broughton estate would come to the church and crack and whirl a huge gad whip at certain points in the service.

Hock Tide (11 April). On this day it was the custom for the women to go out into the streets and roads with cords, and stop and bind all those of the other sex they met, holding them till they purchased their release by a small contribution of money.

Hungerford Hocktide Festival and Tutti Men, Berkshire.

Biddenden Dole, Kent (Easter Monday). All who attend are given a biscuit in the shape of Eliza and Mary Chulkhurst, conjoined twins born in the village during the eleventh century.

St George's Day (23 April). St George, patron saint of England is celebrated at events across the country.

May

May Day – The first day of summer. An ancient British day of celebration including maypole dancing and festivities to pray for the continued fertility of the land and good harvests. In some villages 'Jack in the Green', a fellow bedecked in the sprigs of May, would lead a procession through the streets.

Padstow 'Obby 'Oss Celebrations, Cornwall (1 May).

Flora day, The Furry Dance and Hal-an-Tow ceremonies, Helston, Cornwall (8 May).

Spalding Flower Parade, Lincolnshire.

Garland Day, Abbotsbury, Dorset.

Bampton Morris Dance, Oxfordshire.

Well-Dressing – Burton upon Trent, Tissington and Wirksworth. A ceremony performed to give thanks for pure spring water.

Rochester Dickens Festival, Rochester, Kent. In celebration of the great writer.

Harwich Kichel Throwing (third Thursday in May). The town mayor throws buns from a window into the expectant crowd below.

Weighing the Mayor, High Wycombe, Buckinghamshire (third Saturday in May). Yes, really. A public weighing of the mayor.

Beating the Bounds. Once carried out in every parish across England and Wales.

COTSWOLD GAMES.

Cotswold Olympick Games (held on the Friday after Spring Bank Holiday). Anyone for competitive shin-kicking?

Bolster Day, St Agnes, Cornwall. A re-enactment of the legend of a Cornish giant.

Great Wishford Grovely Ceremony, Wiltshire (29 May).
A celebration of Oak Apple Day (see below).

Oak Apple Day (29 May). The birthday of King Charles II and a day
upon which was celebrated his evasion from capture by hiding in
the Boscobel oak tree after the Battle of Worcester in 1651 and his
eventual restoration to the throne in 1660. Once a public holiday
across England it was formally abolished in 1859 but is still marked
in a few locations, notably the Royal Hospital, Chelsea.

Tetbury Woolsack Race, Gloucestershire.

June
Appleby Horse Fair, Cumbria.

Colchester Oyster Fayre.

The Flitch Trials (every Leap Year) Great Dunmow, Essex. Couples
who in a 'twelvemonth and a day', have not 'wisht themselves
unmarried again' can win a side of bacon.

Midsummer Bonfires, Cornwall.

Filly Loo – a celebration of the longest day – Ashmore, Dorset
(Friday nearest 21 June).

Bawming the Thorn, Appleton Thorn, Warrington, Cheshire. This
takes place on the Saturday closest to Midsummer's Day and involves

the bedecking with ribbons of a thorn tree in the village, followed by children singing and dancing around it. Folklore has it that the hawthorn at Appleton Thorn is the product of a cutting of the Holy Thorn of Glastonbury, which is meant to have grown from the staff of Joseph of Arimathea.

Galashiels Braw Lads Gathering, Borders.

Solstice Celebrations, Stonehenge, Wiltshire (21 June).

July

Ambleside Rushbearing Festival, Cumbria. A procession, church service, sports and fell race (usually first Saturday in July).

Eyemouth Herring Queen Festival, Berwickshire.

Llangollen International Musical Eisteddfod.

Sheringham Lobster Potty Festival, Norfolk.

Horn Fair, Ebernoe, West Sussex (25 July). A celebration and a cricket match.

Marldon Apple Pie Fair, Devon.

International Gilbert and Sullivan Festival, Buxton, Derbyshire.

August
Lammas Day, the Festival of the Gule of August, once celebrated across the land (1 August).

Shrewsbury Flower Show, Shropshire – the world's longest-running flower show.

Worthing International Birdman, Sussex. Competitors create contraptions to assist flight from the end of the pier.

The Burryman – Queensferry, Lothian – A local man is covered in burrs and walked around a 7-mile route. It can take many hours to complete.

The Cowal Highland Gathering (Highland Games), Dunoon.

Grasmere Sports, Cumbria. Includes fell running and Cumberland wrestling.

Burning of Bartle, West Witton, Yorkshire (Saturday nearest 24 August). The burning of an effigy.

Notting Hill Carnival, London.

September
St Giles' Fair, Oxford.

Braemar Royal Highland Gathering, Grampian.

Widecombe Fair, Dartmoor, Devon.

Abbots Bromley Horn Dance, Staffordshire (Monday after first Sunday after 4 September). A medieval dance using antlers.

Egremont Crab Fair, Cumbria – particularly noted for its gurning competition (third Saturday in September).

October
Braughing Old Man's Day (2 October).

Nottingham Goose Fair.

Costermonger's Harvest Festival, St Martin-in-the-Fields, London.

Mop Fair, Tewkesbury, Gloucestershire. A two-day event featuring fairground rides, stalls and games.

Tavistock Goose Fair, Devon.

Taunton Carnival and Cider Barrel Race, Somerset.

All Hallows Eve (31 October) A night of ghosts and ghoulies celebrated across the land.

November
Mischief Night, mostly in Yorkshire and the north (4 November). Pranks and mischief abound in this tradition.

Guy Fawkes Night (5 November). English celebration of the failure of the Gunpowder Plot to blow up the Houses of Parliament commemorated in the rhyme:

Remember, remember the fifth of November
Gunpowder, treason and plot.
I see no reason, why gunpowder treason
Should ever be forgot.

Guy Fawkes, guy, t'was his intent
To blow up king and parliament.
Three score barrels were laid below
To prove old England's overthrow.

By God's mercy he was catch'd
With a darkened lantern and burning match.
So, holler boys, holler boys, Let the bells ring.
Holler boys, holler boys, God save the king!

And what shall we do with him?
Burn him!

Lewes Bonfire Night, East Sussex (5 November), not only marks
Guy Fawkes night but also the memory of the seventeen Protestant
martyrs from the town burned at the stake for their faith during the
Marian Persecutions.

Firing the Fenny Poppers, Fenny Statford, Buckinghamshire (11
November). The ceremonial firing of six small cannon.

December

Mumming Plays were once performed across Great Britain to celebrate the festive season during December.

The Poor Old Hoss, Richmond, Yorkshire (24 December).

Christmas Day (25 December).

Boxing Day (26 December) The traditional day to exchange Christmas boxes or gifts.

Sword Dancing, Flamborough, Humberside.

Pass the Wassail Bowl on Old Year's Night, Scotland (31 December).

Burning the Old Year Out, Biggar, Lanark, and Wick, Caithness (31 December).

Tar-Barrel Ceremony, Allendale, Northumberland (31 December).

Flambeaux Procession, Comrie, Perthshire (31 December).

Fireball Parade, Stonehaven, Kincardineshire (31 December).

UNION FLAG . . . OR IS IT UNION JACK?

Whether the flag of the British nation should be the Union Flag or the Union Jack has been hotly debated over the years. Some claim the flag is only a 'Jack' when flown from a battleship of war, but according to the Flag Institute, the vexillological organisation for the United Kingdom, 'the national flag of the United Kingdom, the Crown Dependencies and Overseas Territories is the Union Flag, which may also be called the Union Jack.' They also point out from early in its life the Admiralty itself frequently referred to the flag as the Union Jack, whatever its use and that in 1902 an Admiralty circular announced that Their Lordships had decided that either name could be used officially.

TEN BRILLIANT BRITISH BRASS BANDS

All winners of the National Brass Band Championships between 1945 and 2008.

Black Dyke Mills
Brighouse and Rastrick
C.W.S. Glasgow
Desford Colliery Caterpillar
Fairey Aviation Works
G.U.S. Footwear
Grimethorpe Colliery
Munn & Felton's Footwear
Wingates Temperance
Yorkshire Imperial Metals

QUINTESSENTIALLY BRITISH CLUBS

Dittons Skiff and Punting Club
Guards Polo Club
Houldsworth Working Men's Club
Marylebone Cricket Club
The British Lawnmower Racing Association
The Club of Thirteen
The English Tiddlywinks Association
The Dangerous Sports Club
The Folklore Society
The Hellfire Club
The Kennel Club
The National Vintage Tractor and Engine Club
The Locomotive Club of Great Britain
The London Omnibus Traction Society
The Lunar Society of Birmingham
The Manchester Universities Guild of Change Ringers
The Ovaltinies Club
The Pony Club
The Ramblers
The Royal Canoe Club
The Royal National Rose Society
The Sealed Knot
The Spalding Gentlemen's Society
The Woolhope Naturalists' Field Club
The Wirral Naturist Club

SOME DISTINCTIVELY BRITISH MAGAZINES AND NEWSLETTERS PAST AND PRESENT

The Letter Box Study Group Newsletter
Narrow Gauge and Industrial Railway Modelling Review
Fortean Times
Heating and Ventilation News
Concrete Quarterly
The Strand Magazine
Fairy Chess Review
Titbits
Fish Friers News
Lilliput Magazine
Angling Times
Family Tree Magazine
Best of British Magazine
People's Friend
Country Life
The Field
Farmers Weekly
The Lady
Horse & Hound
Drain Trader
Fencing and Landscaping News
The Lancet
The Anglo-Saxon Review
John Bull Magazine
Knotting Matters, The Journal of the International Guild of Knot Tyers
Milk Bottle News
Viz
Taxation Magazine
The Chap
The Idler
Occult Review
British Homing World – The most popular pigeon racing weekly
    magazine in the UK.
Private Eye

TWENTY CLASSIC BRITISH MAGAZINES FOR CHILDREN AND YOUNG PEOPLE PAST AND PRESENT

Twinkle
Warlord
Bunty
Beano
Dandy
Eagle
Girl's Own Paper
Boy's Own Paper
The Magnet
The Hornet
Sunny Stories
Enid Blyton's Playways
Look-In
Smash Hits
Jackie
Battle
Misty
Tiger
Whizzer and Chips
The Beezer

THE FIRST TEN WINNERS OF THE 'MISS GREAT BRITAIN' NATIONAL BATHING BEAUTY CONTEST

1945	Lydia Reed, Morecambe and Heysham
1946	June Rivers, Manchester
1947	June Mitchel, Birmingham
1948	Pamela Bayliss, Northern Ireland
1949	Elaine Price, Bolton
1950	Anne Heywood, Birmingham
1951	Marlene Dee, Henley-on-Thames
1952	Doreen Dawne, London
1953	Brenda Mee, Derby
1954	Patricia Butler, Hoylake

PIPE-SMOKER OF THE YEAR

The archetypal British man was one synonymous with his pipe. The competition for Pipe Smoker of the Year was established by the Briar Pipe Trade Association (later renamed the British Pipesmokers' Council) in 1964. Afraid their contest would fall foul of the laws banning the promotion of tobacco, the award was discontinued in 2004. Here is a list of the winners:

1964	Rupert Davies	1983	Patrick Moore
1965	Harold Wilson	1984	Henry Cooper
1966	Andrew Cruickshank	1985	Jimmy Greaves
1967	Warren Mitchell	1986	David Bryant
1968	Peter Cushing	1987	Barry Norman
1969	Jack Hargreaves	1988	Ian Botham
1970	Eric Morecambe	1989	Jeremy Brett
1971	The Rt Hon. Lord	1990	Laurence Marks
	Manny Shinwell	1991	John Harvey-Jones
1973	Frank Muir	1992	Tony Benn
1974	Fred Trueman	1993	Rod Hull
1975	Campbell Adamson	1994	Ranulph Fiennes
1976	Harold Wilson	1995	Jethro (Geoffrey Rowe)
	(Pipeman of the	1996	Colin Davis
	Decade)	1997	Malcolm Bradbury
1977	Brian Barnes	1998	Willie John McBride
1978	Magnus Magnusson	1999	Trevor Baylis
1979	J.B. Priestley	2000	Joss Ackland
1980	Edward Fox	2001	Russ Abbot
1981	James Galway	2002	Richard Dunhill
1982	Dave Lee Travis	2003	Stephen Fry

BEST-DRESSED MAN

The Menswear Association revived the Britain's Best Dressed Man award for men in the public eye in 1979. The first winner was actor Robert Powell, while other finalists for that year included Dave Allen, Roy Castle, John Conteh, Ronnie Corbett, Edward Fox, Mickey Most, Oliver Tobias, Ernie Wise and Mike Yarwood. The following year the winner was footballer Kevin Keegan, closely followed by finalists Larry Grayson, 'Diddy' David Hamilton, Vince Hill, Terry Wogan, Sir Keith Joseph. Also up there for a second year, but pipped at the post again was Roy Castle.

IT'S A KNOCKOUT

One of the most avidly watched television programmes of the 1970s was *It's a Knockout*, presented for most of the decade by Stuart Hall and Eddie Waring (David Vine presented the show from 1967 to 1971). The winning teams from 1972 to 1980 were:

1972	Luton
1973	Ely
1974	Southport
1975	Onchen (Isle of Man)
1976	Blackpool
1977	Macclesfield
1978	Sandwell
1979	Douglas
1980	Kettering

SOME RARE BRITISH SURNAMES

Sallow
Fernsby
Villan
Miracle
Dankworth
Relish
MacQuoid
Loughty
Birdwhistle
Berrycloth
Culpepper

Tumbler
Ajax
Edevane
Gastrell
Slora
Bread
MacCaa
Spinster
Puscat
Bytheseashore (pronounced
    Bitherseeshore)

VERY UNUSUAL (AND UNFORTUNATE) NAMES RECORDED ON BRITISH CENSUS RETURNS OF THE NINETEENTH CENTURY

Isabella Arseman, Cuddesdon, Oxfordshire
William Bastard, Bursledon, Hampshire
Dick Bender, Camberwell, London
Bessy Bent, Market Deeping, Lincolnshire
Arthur Bollock, Great Grimsby, Lincolnshire
Elijah and Emma Boobie, Taunton St James, Somerset

Joseph Bum, Twickenham, Middlesex
Henry and Elizabeth Bummer, Croydon, Surrey
Fanny Cunt, Hastings, St Mary Magdalene, Sussex
Richard Dick, Heworth, Durham
Thomas and Martha Dong, Wisbech St Peter, Cambridgeshire
Harriet Donger, Ipswich, Suffolk
Fanny Felcher, Mayfield, Derbyshire
Watt Fuck, Willington, Northumberland
Amanda Fucker, Newport, Monmouthshire
John Farter, Benwell, Northumberland
Minnie Gobble, Battersea, London
Fanny Humper, St Luke Old Street, Middlesex
Alice Knob, Epsom, Surrey
Isaac Lickass, Easingwold, North Riding of Yorkshire
Michael and Ellen McAnus, Leeds, Yorkshire
Richard and Anne Muppet, Brighton, Sussex
Billy Nobber, East Worlington, Devon
Adolf Pants, Woolwich, London
Elisabeth Plop, Fulham, London
Charles and Emma Plopper, Clerkenwell, London
Henry Penis, Brixton, Surrey
Sarah Pisser, Whitechapel, London
Andrew Queer, Poplar, London
Mark Shitman, Stepney, London
James and Mary Shitter, Corfe Castle, Dorset
Fanny Silly, Brighouse, West Riding of Yorkshire
George Soiler, Sutterton, Lincolnshire
William Tit, Lymington, Hampshire
George and Mary Tosser, Shoreditch St Leonard, Middlesex
Florence Turd, Itchen Ferry, Hampshire
Robert Turdman, Aston Manor, Warwickshire
William Twit, Harrowsley, Lincolnshire
Ernest Urine, Jesmond, Northumberland
Samuel Vomit, Lambeth, London
John Wanker, Tossdyke, Lincolnshire
William Dove Wanker, Towcester, Northamptonshire
James and Florence Wankling, Nottingham, Nottinghamshire
James and Fanny Wankman, Colchester, Essex

. . . And not forgetting the old Orkney family name of Twat.

TEN CLASSIC BRITISH TRACTORS

The Saunderson Model G (1916–24) – best selling tractor of its day.
The David Brown Cropmaster (1947–54)
Allis Chalmers D-270 (1954–7)
Austin R (1919–24)
Field-Marshall (1945–57)
Fordson Major (1945–52)
BMB President (1950–6)
Ferguson 'Fergie' TE 20 (1946–8)
The Massey Ferguson MF 35X Multi-power Diesel Tractor (1962–4)
Nuffield 'Universal' M4 (1948–54)

TEN CLASSIC GREAT BRITISH
VINTAGE LAWNMOWERS

Atco De Luxe N Type
Drummond Willing Worker
Excelsior Monarch
Folbate A1
Lloyd's Autosickle
Mowrite
Qualcast Powered Panther
Ransomes Matador Mk 1
Shanks Jehu
Webb Whippet

TEN CLASSIC ROSES FOUND IN BRITISH COUNTRY GARDENS

Rosa Mundi
Provins Rose
Ispahan
Celestial
William Lobb
Comte de Chambord
Rose du Roi
Old Blush
Roserie de l'Hay
Hansa

COLLECTIVE NOUNS

One of the delights of the English language is the use of collective nouns. Many of them are fanciful and have never had any real currency, while others have been recognised for centuries. Here are a few of the author's favourites:

A business of ferrets
A charm of finches
An exaltation of larks
A watch of nightingales
A tiding of magpies
A hastiness of cooks
A husk of hares
A bevy of quail
A lamentation of swans
A file of civil servants
A gaggle of geese
A grist of bees
A murder of crows
A mischief of rats
A parliament of rooks
A skulk of foxes
A blush of boys
A bench of Bishops
A glaring of cats
A trunkload of clowns

CRUFT'S

The first Cruft's dog show, billed as the 'First Great Terrier Show', was held in 1886 and had 57 classes and 600 entries. The first show to be named 'Cruft's' was 'Cruft's Greatest Dog Show', where all breeds were invited to compete. It was held at the Royal Agricultural Hall, Islington, in 1891.

GENTLEMEN'S CLUBS

When 'in town' a gentleman needs to visit his club. Here are some of them and the dates that they were established:

Army and Navy Club (1837)	36–9 Pall Mall
The Athenaeum (1824)	40 Dover Street
Boodles (1762)	28 St James's Street
Brooks's (1764)	60 St James's Street
Carlton Club (1832)	69 St James's Street
Cavalry and Guards Club (1810)	127 Piccadilly
Eccentric Club (1781, refounded 2008)	40 Dover Street
Garrick Club (1831)	15 Garrick Street
Pratt's (1857)	14 Park Place, St James's
Reform Club (1836)	104–5 Pall Mall
Savage Club (1857)	1 Whitehall Place
Savile Club (1868)	69 Brook Street
Turf Club (1861)	5 Carlton House Terrace
White's Club (1693)	37 St James's Street

13

ON THIS DAY

JANUARY

1 January 1785 – *The Daily Universal Register*, the newspaper that was later renamed *The Times* in 1788, was published for the first time.

2 January 1727 – Major General James Wolfe, vaunted for his victory over the French in Canada during the Seven Years War, was born at Westerham, Kent.

3 January 1882 – William Harrison Ainsworth, the historical novelist who brought thrilling semi-fictional tales of highwayman Dick Turpin, criminal and gaol-breaker Jack Sheppard and many others to Victorian audiences, died at Reigate in Surrey.

4 January 871 – The Battle of Reading is a victory for the Viking forces over the West Saxons led by Ethelred of Wessex and Alfred the Great.

5 January 1944 – The *Daily Mail* became the first transoceanic newspaper.

6 January 1781 – The Battle of Jersey. British forces defeat the last attempt by France to invade the Channel Island of Jersey.

7 January 1927 – The first transatlantic telephone service is established between New York and London.

8 January 1824 – Wilkie Collins, author of *The Woman in White* and *The Moonstone*, was born at 11 New Cavendish Street, Marylebone, London.

9 January 1768 – Philip Astley stages the first modern circus in London.

10 January 1861 – The first section of the London Underground opens between Paddington station and Farringdon station.

11 January 1569 – The first recorded lottery in England was drawn.

12 January 1895 – The National Trust was founded by Octavia Hill, Sir Robert Hunter and the Very Revd Hardwicke Canon Rawnsley.

13 January 1842 – Dr William Brydon, an assistant surgeon in the British East India Company Army during the First Anglo-Afghan War, became famous for being the sole survivor of an army of 4,500 men and 12,000 camp followers when he reaches the safety of a garrison in Jalalabad, Afghanistan.

14 January 1904 – Cecil Beaton, one of Britain's greatest fashion and portrait photographers, was born in Hampstead.

15 January 1759 – The British Museum was opened to the public in its first home of Montagu House in Bloomsbury.

16 January 1707 – The Scottish Parliament ratified the Act of Union, paving the way for the creation of Great Britain.

17 January 1912 – Captain Robert Falcon Scott RN and five members of his expedition reached the South Pole, only to find that they had been beaten to it a month earlier by a Norwegian expedition led by Roald Amundsen.

18 January 1788 – The first elements of the First Fleet carrying 736 convicts from England to Australia arrived at Botany Bay.

19 January 1915 – The first bombs dropped by a Zeppelin in an offensive raid over Great Britain fell on Norfolk.

20 January 1936 – King George V died at Sandringham, Norfolk.

21 January 1924 – Saucy comedian Benny Hill was born Alfred Hawthorne Hill in Southampton.

22 January 1901 – HM Queen Victoria died at 6.30 p.m. at Osborne House on the Isle of Wight.

23 January 1879 – Second and final day of the Battle of Rorke's Drift during the Zulu War. Just over 150 British soldiers of the 24th Foot and colonial troops successfully defended the garrison and repelled a force of between 3,000–4,000 Zulu warriors. Eleven Victoria Crosses were awarded for this single action.

24 January 1908 – The first Boy Scout troop was organised in England by national hero Lieutenant-General Robert Baden-Powell.

25 January 1759 – Robert Burns, poet, lyricist and Scotland's favourite son, was born in Ayr.

26 January 1885 – Major-General Charles George Gordon, remembered simply as 'Gordon of Khartoum', was killed around dawn fighting the warriors of the Mahdi in Khartoum, Sudan.

27 January 1944 – Pink Floyd drummer and songwriter Nick Mason was born Nicholas Berkley Mason in Edgbaston, Birmingham.

28 January 1547 – Henry VIII died at the Palace of Whitehall.

29 January 1737 – Tom Paine, author of such tomes as *Common Sense* (1776) and *The Rights of Man* (1791), pamphleteer, radical, inventor, intellectual, revolutionary, and one of the Founding Fathers of the United States, was born in Thetford, Norfolk.

30 January 1649 – The execution of King Charles I.

31 January 1956 – John Joseph Lydon, who under the stage name of Johnny Rotten became lead singer of the influential punk rock band the Sex Pistols, was born in London.

FEBRUARY

1 February 1975 – Richard Wattis, the face of British officialdom on TV and film throughout the 1950s and '60s – from *St Trinians* to Carry On films – passed away in Kensington.

2 February 1461 – The Battle of Mortimer's Cross was a decisive victory for the Yorkists during the Wars of the Roses.

3 February 1960 – Prime Minister Harold Macmillan spoke of 'a wind of change' in a speech to the Parliament of South Africa in Cape Town heralding his Government's likely support for decolonisation.

4 February 1915 – Beloved English comic actor Norman Wisdom was born in Marylebone. His unique brand of slapstick comedy, often directed against authority figures, was very popular in central Europe and he was literally idolised in Albania.

5 February 1920 – Classic English comedy writer, television wit and personality Frank Muir was born in his grandmother's pub, the Derby Arms, in Ramsgate.

6 February 1922 – Patrick Macnee, the actor best known for his portrayal of the quintessential English gentleman and secret agent in the TV series *The Avengers*, was born in Paddington.

7 February 1301 – Edward of Caernarvon (later King Edward II of England) became the first English Prince of Wales.

8 February 1587 – Mary Queen of Scots was executed at Fotheringhay Castle.

9 February 1964 – The Beatles made their first appearance on *The Ed Sullivan Show* in the USA, performing before a record audience of 73 million viewers.

10 February 1906 – The HMS *Dreadnought*, the first all iron-clad, all big gun, turbine-driven battleship, was christened and launched by King Edward VII. Britannia truly ruled the waves!

11 February 1938 – BBC Television produced the world's first ever science fiction television program, an adaptation of a section of the Karel Capek play *R.U.R.*, that coined the term 'robot'.

12 February 1809 – Charles Darwin was born at his family home of The Mount in Shrewsbury.

13 February 1728 – John Hunter was born at Long Calderwood, East Kilbride. Hunter became regarded as one of the most distinguished scientists and surgeons of his day. His collection of specimens formed the basis of the Hunterian Museum at the Royal College of Surgeons and the Hunterian Society of London was named in his honour.

14 February 1852 – Great Ormond St Hospital for Sick Children was founded in London. It was the first hospital providing in-patient beds specifically for children in the English-speaking world.

15 February 1971 – 'Decimal Day' – Britain bade a final farewell to pounds, shillings and pence and the decimalisation of British coinage was completed.

16 February 1923 – English Egyptologist Howard Carter opened the tomb of King Tutankhamun and revealed to the world the best-preserved and most intact pharaonic tomb ever found in the Valley of the Kings, Egypt.

17 February 1930 – Ruth Rendell, crime, psychological thriller and murder mystery writer, and creator of the popular Inspector Wexford series, was born Ruth Grasemann in South Woodford, London.

18 February 1929 – Prolific thriller and military history writer, creator of *The IPCRESS file*, Len Deighton was born in Marylebone, London.

19 February 1819 – British explorer William Smith discovered the South Shetland Islands (a group of islands, lying about 75 miles north of the Antarctic Peninsula) and claimed them in the name of King George III.

20 February 1940 – Footballer and TV soccer pundit Jimmy Greaves was born in Manor Park, East Ham.

21 February 1804 – The first self-propelling steam locomotive (built by Richard Trevithick) made its first appearance in trials on the Pen-y-Darren Ironworks tramroad in Wales.

22 February 1928 – Popular TV game show host, comedian, singer and dancer Bruce Forsyth was born in Edmonton, London.

23 February 1908 – John Mills, star of such classic British films as *Great Expectations* (1946), *The Colditz Story* (1955), *Above Us The Waves* (1955), *Ice Cold in Alex* (1958) and *Tunes of Glory* (1960) was born Lewis Ernest Watts Mills in North Elmham, Norfolk.

24 February 1711 – The London première of *Rinaldo* by Handel, the first Italian opera written for the London stage.

25 February 1797 – Irish-American Colonel William Tate and his force of 1,000–1,500 soldiers of La Legion Noire surrendered after the Battle of Fishguard – the last attempted invasion of Great Britain.

26 February 1935 – Robert Watson Watt and his assistant Arnold Wilkins demonstrated the principles of bouncing radio waves off aircraft at Daventry – an idea that led to the creation of RADAR.

27 February 1939 – Borley Rectory in Essex, described by paranormal researcher Harry Price as 'the most haunted house in England' and the subject of many books, was gutted by fire.

28 February 1900 – The Relief of Ladysmith during the Second Boer War took place.

29 February – Leap Day! – 1928 – Stage, screen and radio actor Joss Ackland was born Sidney Edmond Jocelyn Ackland in North Kensington, London.

MARCH

1 March 1980 – Football legend William Ralph 'Dixie' Dean, the man who scored seven hat-tricks in the 1927/28 season and achieved a record-breaking 60 league goals in 39 games, died in Liverpool aged 73.

2 March 1797 – The Bank of England issued the first £1 bank note.

3 March 1958 – Versatile television, stage and film actress Miranda Richardson, best known for her portrayal of Queen Elizabeth I 'Queenie' in *Blackadder II*, was born in Southport.

4 March 1936 – Lotus driving legend and Formula One world championship winner (1963 and 1965) Jim Clarke was born in Fife.

5 March 1936 – First flight of the Spitfire prototype aircraft flown by Vickers Aviation chief test pilot, Captain Joseph 'Mutt' Summers, at Eastleigh Aerodrome, Hampshire.

6 March 1707 – The Act of Union – Scotland and England were unified.

7 March 1876 – Scottish inventor Alexander Graham Bell was granted a patent for an invention which he called 'the telephone'. He made the first successful telephone call on 10 March 1876, the words spoken were: 'Mr Watson, come here, I want to see you.'

8 March 1859 – Kenneth Grahame, the creator of such beloved children's storybook characters as Ratty, Mole, Toad and Badger in his book *The Wind in the Willows* (1908), was born in Edinburgh.

9 March 1915 – 'Johnnie' Johnson, Britain's No. 1 fighter pilot ace of the Second World War with 34 claimed victories over enemy aircraft, seven shared victories and three shared probables, was born James Edgar Johnson at Barrow upon Soar, Leicestershire.

10 March 1801 – The first modern census of the United Kingdom was conducted.

11 March 1702 – England's first national daily newspaper the *Daily Courant*, was published for the first time.

12 March 1881 – Andrew Watson made his Scotland debut as the world's first black Association Football player to play at international level.

13 March 1942 – Geoffrey Hayes, the main man in the popular children's TV show *Rainbow*, was born in Stockport.

14 March 1885 – Comic opera *The Mikado* by Gilbert and Sullivan, had its first public performance at the Savoy Theatre in London and ran for 672 performances.

15 March 1923 – Journalist and broadcaster Charles Wheeler, the BBC's longest-serving foreign correspondent, was born in Berlin, where his father was working for the British Council.

16 March 1872 – Wanderers became the first winners of the FA Cup, beating Royal Engineers 1–0 at The Oval.

17 March 1337 – Edward, the Black Prince was made Duke of Cornwall, the first Duchy in England.

18 March 1893 – First World War poet Wilfred Edward Salter Owen was born near Oswestry, Shropshire.

19 March 1649 – The House of Commons passed an act abolishing the House of Lords, declaring it 'useless and dangerous to the people of England.'

20 March 1908 – Stage, film and television actor Michael Redgrave, whose film appearances include such classics as *The Lady Vanishes* (1938), *The Importance of Being Earnest* (1952), *The Dam Busters* (1955) and *The Heroes of Telemark* (1965), was born in Bristol.

21 March 1999 – Bristol-born Brian Jones and his Swiss co-pilot Bertrand Piccard were the first to complete a non-stop balloon flight around the world on board *Breitling Orbiter 3*.

22 March 1945 – Allied forces began crossing the Rhine and the end of the Third Reich was in sight.

23 March 1935 – Comedian, scriptwriter and popular TV and radio panellist Barry Cryer was born in Leeds.

24 March 1707 – The Acts of Union were signed, officially uniting the Kingdoms of England and Scotland to create the Kingdom of Great Britain.

25 March 1306 – Robert the Bruce became King of Scotland.

26 March 1839 – The first Henley Regatta was proposed by Captain Edmund Gardiner at a public meeting in Henley town hall.

27 March 1871 – The first international rugby football match was played between England and Scotland at Raeburn Place in Edinburgh.

28 March 1964 – 'Pirate' Radio Caroline commenced regular broadcasts.

29 March 1461 – The Battle of Towton, Yorkshire, described by some historians as 'the largest and bloodiest battle ever fought on English soil', saw Edward of York defeat the belligerents of the House of Lancaster to become King Edward IV of England.

30 March 2002 – Death of Queen Elizabeth, the Queen Mother, aged 101.

31 March 1809 – Edward FitzGerald, poet and writer best known for completing the first English translation of *The Rubaiyat of Omar Khayyam*, was born in Bredfield, Suffolk.

APRIL

1 April 1957 – Britain has enjoyed many press and TV pranks on 'April Fool's Day' probably the most notorious being the spoof BBC documentary about spaghetti crops in Switzerland which was aired on this day.

2 April 1962 – The first official Panda crossing was opened outside Waterloo station, London.

3 April 1933 – The first flight over Mount Everest was achieved by a British expedition, led by Squadron Leader Douglas Douglas-Hamilton, the Marquis of Clydesdale flying a Westland PV-3 biplane.

4 April 1873 – The Kennel Club was founded as a result of a meeting held at 2 Albert Mansions, Victoria Street, London, on this day.

5 April 1804 – The first recorded meteorite to fall on Scotland landed near High Possil on the northern outskirts of Glasgow.

6 April 1320 – The Declaration of Arbroath, intended as a confirmation of Scotland's status as an independent, sovereign state that defended the right to use military force if unjustly attacked, was submitted as a letter to Pope John XXII.

7 April 1770 – Romantic poet and Poet Laureate, William Wordsworth, was born in Cockermouth, Cumbria.

8 April 1941 – Doyenne of British fashion Vivienne Westwood was born Vivienne Isabel Swire in the village of Tintwistle, Derbyshire.

9 April 1806 – Isambard Kingdom Brunel was born in Portsmouth, Hampshire.

10 April 1633 – The first recorded shop window display of bananas was made in Thomas Johnson's store in London.

11 April 1689 – William III and Mary II were crowned as joint sovereigns of Britain.

12 April 1606 – The Union Flag was adopted as the national flag of Great Britain.

13 April 1771 – Mining engineer, inventor and steam pioneer Richard Trevithick was born in Tregajorran, Cornwall.

14 April 1912 – The RMS *Titanic* hit an iceberg in the North Atlantic at 11.40 p.m. The ship sank the following morning with the loss of 1,514 lives.

15 April 1755 – Samuel Johnson published *A Dictionary of the English Language*. Johnson's work was seen as the pre-eminent English dictionary for the next 173 years and was only surpassed from that time by the *Oxford English Dictionary*.

16 April 1889 – Silent film star and director Charlie Chaplin was born Charles Spencer Chaplin on East Street, Walworth, London.

17 April 1725 – John Rudge bequeathed 20*s* a year to the parish of Trysull in Staffordshire that a poor man might be employed to go about the church during the sermon to keep the people awake and to keep dogs out of the church.

18 April 1899 – The St Andrew's Ambulance Association was granted a Royal Charter by Queen Victoria.

19 April 1770 – Captain James Cook sighted the eastern coast of what is now Australia, which he named New South Wales and claimed for Great Britain.

20 April 1924 – The irrepressibly suave actor Leslie Phillips, star of such classic comedies as *Carry on Nurse*, *The Navy Lark* and *Doctor in Love*, was born in Tottenham, London.

21 April 1934 – The 'Surgeon's Photograph' the most famous photo allegedly showing the Loch Ness Monster, was published in the *Daily Mail*.

22 April 1969 – British yachtsman Robin Knox-Johnston completed the first solo non-stop circumnavigation of the world.

23 April 303 – St George was martyred.

24 April 1922 – The first section of the Imperial Wireless Chain providing wireless telegraphy between Leafield in Oxfordshire and Cairo in Egypt came into operation.

25 April 1599 – Oliver Cromwell was born in Huntingdon.

26 April 1564 – William Shakespeare's baptism was recorded in the Parish Register of Holy Trinity Church at Stratford-upon-Avon.

27 April 1908 – Opening ceremony of the first Olympics to be held in Great Britain at the White City Stadium, London.

28 April 1772 – A goat that had twice circumnavigated the globe died at Mile End, London. First, in the discovery ship *Dolphin*, under Captain Wallis, and secondly, in the renowned *Endeavour*, under Captain Cook. Just previous to her death, the Lords of the Admiralty had signed a warrant, admitting her to the privileges of an in-pensioner of Greenwich Hospital.

29 April 1745 – Cowper Thornhill, the keeper of the Bell Inn at Stilton, set out from his house at four in the morning, and arrived at the Queen's Arms in Shoreditch, London, in three hours and fifty-two minutes. He returned to Stilton again in four hours and twelve minutes and came back to London again in four hours and thirteen minutes – all for a wager of 500 guineas. He was allowed fifteen hours to perform the feat that would cover a total of 213 miles, and achieved it in twelve hours and seventeen minutes. It was regarded as the greatest riding achievement of the age.

30 April 1933 – Richard 'Dickie' Davis presenter of ITV's *World of Sport,* a feature of Saturday lunch times and afternoons from 1968 to 1985, was born in Wallasey, Merseyside.

MAY

1 May 1840 – The Penny Black postage stamp became the world's first adhesive postage stamp to be used in a public postal system.

2 May 1611 – The King James Bible was published for the first time in London by printer Robert Barker.

3 May 1951 – The Royal Festival Hall opened in London as part of the Festival of Britain.

4 May 1471 – The Battle of Tewkesbury took place and was a decisive victory for the Yorkist forces led by Edward IV and Richard of Gloucester.

5 May 2011 – Claude Choules, the last British combat veteran of the First World War, died aged 110. Choules was a career serviceman of the Royal Navy. He was also the last veteran to have served in both world wars, the last surviving seaman from the First World War and the last military witness to the scuttling of the German fleet in Scapa Flow.

6 May 1954 – Roger Bannister became the first person to run the mile in under 4 minutes at Iffley Road Track in Oxford. He achieved his feat in 3 minutes 59.4 seconds.

7 May 1916 – Huw Wheldon, television presenter and executive best remembered for his arts programme *Monitor*, was born in Prestatyn.

8 May 1945 – VE (Victory in Europe) Day was celebrated across Britain to mark the unconditional surrender of the German armed forces and the end of Hitler's Third Reich.

9 May 1671 – Captain Thomas Blood attempted to steal the Crown Jewels from the Tower of London.

10 May 1940 – The first attack on England's mainland during the Second World War was officially recorded as taking place at 4.00 a.m. when 23 incendiary bombs fell on East Stour Farm, Chilham, near Canterbury in Kent.

11 May 1892 – English character actress Margaret Rutherford, best remembered for her film performances as Miss Marple in the 1960s, was born in Balham, London.

12 May 1926 – End of the General Strike.

13 May 1842 – Sir Arthur Sullivan, one half of Victorian comic opera supremos Gilbert and Sullivan, was born in Lambeth.

14 May 1926 – Eric Morecambe, comedian, entertainer and one half of the double act Morecambe and Wise, was born John Eric Bartholomew in Morecambe, Lancashire.

15 May 1718 – Norwich-born London lawyer and inventor James Puckle patented his 'Defence Gun' capable of firing up to nine rounds a minute – arguably this was the world's first machine gun.

16 May 1943 – Bombers of 617 Squadron RAF flew out from Scampton in Lincolnshire to attack the Möhne, Eder and Sorpe Dams in Operation Chastise and entered history as 'The Dam Busters'.

17 May 1749 – Edward Jenner, physician, scientist, pioneer of the smallpox vaccine and 'the father of immunology' was born in Berkeley, Gloucestershire.

18 May 1909 – Tennis champion Fred Perry was born in Stockport.

19 May 1536 – Queen Anne Boleyn, second wife of Henry VIII, was executed for treason on Tower Green. She knelt upright and her head was removed with a single deft swipe of the blade from a sword wielded by a headsman brought from Calais at her request.

20 May 1609 – Shakespeare's sonnets were published in London by Thomas Thorpe who entered the book in the Stationers' Register on this day.

21 May 1894 – The official opening of the Manchester Ship Canal was performed by HM Queen Victoria.

22 May 1907 – Laurence Olivier, one of the greatest British stage and film actors of the twentieth century, was born in Dorking, Surrey.

23 May 1918 – Patrick Cargill, a typical English gentleman character actor, a familiar face on comedy programmes in the 1960s and '70s, best remembered for *Father, Dear Father*, was born at Bexhill-on-Sea.

24 May 1924 – Radio, TV and film comedy legend Tony Hancock was born Anthony John Hancock on Southam Road, Hall Green, Birmingham.

25 May 1913 – Richard Dimbleby, one of the greatest figures in British broadcasting history, was born Frederick Richard Dimbleby near Richmond.

26 May 1904 – George Formby, comedy actor and singer-songwriter famed for his cheeky performances with his ukulele was born George Hoy Booth in Wigan, Lancashire.

27 May 1922 – Christopher Frank Carandini Lee was born in Belgravia, London. Despite performing roles in 275 films since 1946, making him the Guinness World Record holder for most film acting roles ever, he remains best known for his portrayal of Dracula in Hammer Horror films.

28 May 1908 – Ian Fleming, the creator of James Bond and *Chitty Chitty Bang Bang* (1964), was born at 27 Green Street, Mayfair.

29 May 1781 – John Walker, the inventor of the friction match, was born at Stockton-on-Tees.

30 May 1963 – Helen Sharman, the first Briton in space, was born in Grenoside, Sheffield.

31 May 1669 – Samuel Pepys recorded the last event in his diary. He stated, 'And thus ends all that I doubt I shall ever be able to do with my own eyes in the keeping of my journal, I being not able to do it any longer, having done now so long as to undo my eyes almost every time that I take a pen in my hand.' He concluded with the lines: 'And so I betake myself to that course, which is almost as much as to see myself go into my grave: for which, and all the discomforts that will accompany my being blind, the good God prepare me!'

JUNE

1 June 1794 – 'The Glorious First of June' was the first and largest fleet action of the naval conflict between the British Channel Fleet under Admiral Lord Howe and the French Atlantic Fleet during the French Revolutionary War.

2 June 1910 – Charles Rolls, co-founder of Rolls-Royce Limited, became the first man to make a non-stop double crossing of the English Channel by aeroplane.

3 June 1953 – The Coronation of HM Queen Elizabeth II, a day of national celebration and street parties.

4 June 1913 – Suffragette Emily Wilding Davison walked out onto the racecourse and attempted to fasten suffragette colours to King George V's horse, Anmer, at the Epsom Derby. She was trampled, never regained consciousness and died four days later in Epsom Cottage Hospital.

5 June 1916 – British national hero and Secretary of State for War Field Marshal Earl Kitchener of Khartoum was drowned when the armoured cruiser he was travelling aboard, HMS *Hampshire*, struck a mine off the Orkney Islands and sank with the loss of 643 of the 655 members of Kitchener's staff and ship's crew.

6 June 1944 – D-Day – British and Allied forces landed on the beaches of Normandy to begin the liberation of North Western Europe from the forces of the Third Reich.

7 June 1906 – Cunard Line's RMS *Lusitania* was launched at the John Brown Shipyard, Glasgow (Clydebank).

8 June 1949 – George Orwell's novel *Nineteen Eighty-Four* was published.

9 June 1870 – Charles Dickens, one of the greatest authors and social commentators of his day and creator of such books as *The Adventures of Oliver Twist (1839)*, *A Christmas Carol* (1843) and *David Copperfield* (1850), died at his home of Gad's Hill Place in Higham, Kent.

10 June 1829 – The first Boat Race between the Oxford University Boat Club and the Cambridge University Boat Club took place at Henley-on-Thames.

11 June 1847 – Lincolnshire-born Arctic explorer Rear Admiral Sir John Franklyn died while searching for the Northwest Passage. Both expedition ships, the *Erebus* and *Terror,* had become icebound and eventually the entire crew were lost to starvation, hypothermia, tuberculosis, lead poisoning and scurvy.

12 June 1920 – Peter Jones, actor, screenwriter, broadcaster and the voice of The Book in the original radio series and TV adaptation of Douglas Adams' *Hitchhiker's Guide to the Galaxy,* was born in Wem, Shropshire.

13 June 1893 – Lord Peter Wimsey's creator Dorothy L. (Leigh) Sayers was born at in the Head Master's House, Christ Church Cathedral, Oxford.

14 June 1645 – Battle of Naseby. The main army of King Charles I led by the king and Prince Rupert of the Rhine was destroyed by the Parliamentarian New Model Army commanded by Sir Thomas Fairfax and Oliver Cromwell.

15 June 1215 – King John attached his Great Seal to the Magna Carta in the meadow at Runnymede.

16 June 1900 – Arthur Askey, popular radio, film and TV comedian, actor and true all-rounder in the music hall tradition, known for his catchphrase 'Hello playmates!' was born on Moses Street, Liverpool.

17 June 1497 – The Battle of Deptford Bridge. Cornish rebels by led Michael An Gof were defeated by troops led by King Henry VII.

18 June 1815 – The Battle of Waterloo heralded the final defeat of Napoleon Bonaparte by the British, Dutch and German forces under the overall command of the Duke of Wellington.

19 June 1999 – The wedding of Prince Edward, Earl of Wessex and Sophie Rhys-Jones took place.

20 June 1649 – Executioner Richard Brandon, the man believed to have carried out the beheading of Charles I, died at his home on Rosemary Lane, London.

21 June 1916 – Joseph Cyril Bamford, the founder of the heavy plant machinery manufacturing company JCB, was born in Uttoxeter.

22 June 1911 – Coronation of HM King George V and Queen Mary.

23 June 1757 – The Battle of Plassey in Bengal where 3,000 British and Imperial troops under Robert Clive defeated a 50,000-strong Indian army.

24 June 1509 – Coronation of King Henry VIII.

25 June 1900 – Lord Louis 'Dickie' Mountbatten, Supreme Allied Commander South East Asia Command (October 1943–6) and the last Viceroy of India was born at Frogmore House, Windsor.

26 June 1857 – Queen Victoria presented the first Victoria Crosses to 62 recipients who received their award for gallantry during the Crimean War in a special ceremony in Hyde Park.

27 June 1742 – The Battle of Dettingen in Bavaria during the War of the Austrian Succession took place. It was the last time that a British monarch (in this case George II) personally led his troops into battle.

28 June 1838 – Coronation of HM Queen Victoria. She would reign for a total of of 63 years and 7 months.

29 June 1861 – Death of Durham-born poet Elizabeth Barrett Browning, the author of 'How do I love Thee?'

30 June 1894 – Tower Bridge, one of the truly iconic symbols of London, was opened by the Prince of Wales (the future King Edward VII).

JULY

1 July 1916 – First Day of the Battle of the Somme. 60,000 British casualties.

2 July1644 – The Battle of Marston Moor. The combined forces of the Scottish Covenanters under the Earl of Leven and the English Parliamentarians under Lord Fairfax and the Earl of Manchester defeated the Royalists commanded by Prince Rupert and the Marquess of Newcastle.

3 July 1792 – Neoclassical architect, interior and furniture designer Robert Adam was born in Kirkcaldy, Fife.

4 July1865 – Lewis Carroll's children's classic *Alice's Adventures in Wonderland* was published by Macmillian and Co. of London, with 42 captivating illustrations by John Tenniel.

5 July 1954 – The BBC broadcast its first television news bulletin.

6 July 1189 – Richard I 'the Lionheart' was crowned King of England.

7 July 1944 – Tony Jacklin, the most successful European Ryder Cup captain to date and one of the greatest golfers of his age, was born in Scunthorpe.

8 July 1934 – Comedian and comedy writer Marty Feldman was born in the East End of London.

9 July 1877 – The opening day of the first ever Wimbledon Tennis Tournament.

10 July 1645 – The Battle of Langport, near Yeovil, during the English Civil War. Parliamentarian forces led by Sir Thomas Fairfax gained a victory against Royalist forces led by Lord Goring.

11 July 1848 – Waterloo station in London opened as Waterloo Bridge station, named after the nearby bridge that spans the Thames.

12 July 1730 – Notable pottery and earthenware innovator and manufacturer Josiah Wedgwood was born at Burslem in Staffordshire.

13 July 1919 – The British airship R34 lands at Pulham airship station in Norfolk, completing the first airship return journey across the Atlantic in a total of 182 hours of flight.

14 July 1911 – Terry-Thomas, the greatest British film cad and rotter, was born Thomas Terry Hoar-Stevens in Finchley, North London.

15 July 1099 – Christian soldiers took the Church of the Holy Sepulchre in Jerusalem during the First Crusade.

16 July 1723 – Joshua Reynolds, first President of the Royal Academy of Arts, was born in Plympton, Devon.

17 July 1717 – Handel's *Water Music* was given its premiere, performed by 50 musicians on a barge on the Thames as King George I and some of his friends sailed nearby on the Royal Barge.

18 July 1389 – The Truce of Leulinghem was agreed by the Kingdom of France and the Kingdom of England. The truce held for thirteen years – the longest period of sustained peace during the Hundred Years War.

19 July 1843 – The SS *Great Britain*, designed by Isambard Kingdom Brunel, the first screw-propelled oceangoing passenger steamship with an iron hull, was launched at Bristol and became, by far, the largest vessel afloat in the world at that time.

20 July 1938 – Diana Rigg, best known for her portrayal of Emma Peel in the cult 1960s TV show *The Avengers*, was born in Doncaster.

21 July 1934 – Jonathan Miller, theatre and opera director, author, television presenter and member of the comedy revue *Beyond the Fringe*, was born in London.

22 July 1797 – British and Spanish naval forces clash in the Battle of Santa Cruz de Tenerife. Rear-Admiral Nelson received a musket ball shot just above his right elbow and the ship's surgeon had no option but to amputate the forearm.

23 July 1690 – Richard Gibson, the court dwarf to Charles I, died aged 75.

24 July 1927 – Opening of the Menin Gate Memorial to the Missing in Ypres, Belgium. It commemorates, by name, over 54,000 British and Commonwealth soldiers who were killed in the Ypres Salient during the First World War.

25 July 1603 – James VI of Scotland was crowned as King James I of England.

26 July 1945 – The remarkable English actress Helen Mirren was born Helen Lydia Mironoff (her father was Russian in origin and her mother was English) at Queen Charlotte's Hospital, Chiswick, West London.

27 July 1865 – Welsh settlers arrived at Chubut in Argentina.

28 July 1866 – Beatrix Potter, children's author, illustrator and one of the founders of the National Trust, was born at 2 Bolton Gardens, South Kensington.

29 July 1945 – The BBC launched the Light Programme on the radio.

30 July 1966 – England won the World Cup when they beat West Germany 4–2 after extra time at Wembley Stadium.

31 July 1703 – Daniel Defoe was placed in a pillory for the crime of seditious libel after publishing a politically satirical pamphlet but the crowd were sympathetic to him and instead of mud and revolting matter, he was pelted with flowers.

AUGUST

1 August 1759 – The Battle of Minden during the Seven Years' War. An Anglo-German army, commanded by Field Marshal Ferdinand, Duke of Brunswick, was victorious over the French.

2 August 1897 – Major-General Sir Bindon Blood relieved the beleaguered Malakand Field Force and ended the Siege of Malakand on the North West Frontier during the Afghan War.

3 August 1887 – Rupert Brooke, the poet who gave us 'The Old Vicarage, Grantchester' and 'The Soldier', was born at 5 Hillmorton Road in Rugby.

4 August 1914 – The outbreak of the First World War was announced across the country at 11.00 p.m. – celebrations were held in the streets in many places.

5 August 910 – The Battle of Tettenhall (now Wolverhampton) resulted in the defeat of the last Viking invader army by King Edward of Wessex.

6 August 1937 – Barbara Windsor, queen of the Carry On films, was born Barbara Ann Deeks in Shoreditch, London.

7 August 1860 – Alan Leo, the man considered by many to be 'the father of modern astrology', was born William Frederick Allen in Westminster.

8 August 1963 – 'The Great Train Robbery' of £2.6 million (the equivalent of around £40 million today) from a Royal Mail train took place in Buckinghamshire.

9 August 1588 – As England prepared to repel the anticipated invasion by the Spanish Armada, Queen Elizabeth I delivered her inspiring speech in which she declared: 'I know I have the body but of a weak and feeble woman; but I have the heart and stomach of a king, and of a king of England too' to her troops at Tilbury.

10 August 991 – The Battle of Maldon. Anglo-Saxon troops, led by Byrhtnoth, Ealdorman of Essex, were defeated by a band of Viking raiders near Maldon in Essex.

11 August 1994 – Peter Cushing, the English actor best remembered for his appearances in Hammer Horror films, passed away in Whitstable, Kent.

12 August 1880 – Marguerite Radclyffe-Hall, poet and author best known for the classic lesbian novel *The Well of Loneliness* (1928), was born at Sunny Lawn, Durley Road, Bournemouth.

13 August 1964 – Last men to be executed in England – murderers Peter Anthony Allen, at Walton Prison in Liverpool, and Gwynne Owen Evans, at Strangeways Prison in Manchester.

14 August 1888 – A recording of Arthur Sullivan's *The Lost Chord*, one of the first recordings of music ever made, was played during a press conference to introduce Thomas Edison's phonograph in London.

15 August 1945 – VJ (Victory in Japan) Day celebrated to mark the unconditional surrender of Japan and the end of the Second World War.

16 August 1897 – The Tate Gallery in London was opened to the public.

17 August 1926 – Jazz and blues singer, critic and writer George Melly was born Alan George Heywood Melly in Liverpool.

18 August 1925 – Science fiction author Brian Aldiss was born in East Dereham, Norfolk.

19 August 1745 – Prince Charles Edward Stuart raised his standard at Glenfinnan, claiming the Scottish and the English thrones in the name of his father James Stuart. It heralded the beginning of the Jacobite Rebellion that would become known to history as 'the 45'.

20 August 1858 – Charles Darwin published his theory of evolution through natural selection in *The Journal of the Proceedings of the Linnean Society of London.*

21 August 1689 – Battle of Dunkeld, part of the first Jacobite rising, was fought in the streets around Dunkeld Cathedral. Jacobite clans supporting the deposed King James VII of Scotland were defeated by a Scottish government regiment of covenanters who supported William of Orange, King of Scotland.

22 August 1485 – The Battle of Bosworth Field saw a decisive Lancastrian victory, the death of Richard III, the end of the House of Plantagenet, the end of the Wars of the Roses and the ascent of the House of Tudor to the throne.

23 August 1650 – Colonel George Monck formed Monck's Regiment of Foot; it would later become the Coldstream Guards.

24 August 1957 – National treasure Stephen Fry was born in Hampstead, London.

25 August 1930 – Best loved James Bond 007 actor Sean Connery was born Thomas Sean Connery at Fountainbridge, Edinburgh.

26 August 1346 – The Battle of Crécy. An Anglo-Welsh army led by Edward III wins a decisive victory against Philip VI of France.

27 August 1886 – Eric Coates, composer of the theme for *The Dam Busters* (1954), was born at Hucknall, Nottingham.

28 August 1640 – The Battle of Newburn, Northumberland. A Scottish Covenanter army led by General Alexander Leslie defeated an English army under Edward, Lord Conway.

29 August 1833 – The United Kingdom passed legislation for the abolition of slavery across the British Empire.

30 August 1799 – The Dutch fleet was captured by British forces under the command of Sir Ralph Abercromby and Admiral Sir Charles Mitchell.

31 August 1422 – Henry VI became King of England when he was just nine months old, making him the youngest person ever to succeed to the English throne.

SEPTEMBER

1 September 1939 – Operation Pied Piper began. It involved the evacuation of 3 million people, many of them children, from British cities to places of safety in the countryside away from the anticipated enemy bombing raids.

2 September 1666 – Fire broke out on Pudding Lane and rapidly spread to become the Great Fire of London.

3 September 1939 – Prime Minister Neville Chamberlain declared the outbreak of the Second World War at 11.00 a.m.

4 September 1939 – A Bristol Blenheim became the first British aircraft to cross the German coast following the declaration of war.

5 September 1666 – End of the Great Fire of London. The conflagration destroyed 13,200 houses, 87 parish churches and the wooden St Paul's Cathedral.

6 September 1620 – Over 100 pilgrims set sail from Plymouth bound for America aboard the *Mayflower*.

7 September 1913 – Anthony Quayle, who has provided superb performances as a supporting actor in such films as *Anne of a Thousand Days* (1969), *The Battle of the River Plate* (1956), *The Guns of Navarone* (1961) and *Ice Cold in Alex* (1958), was born in Ainsdale, Southport.

8 September 1925 – Peter Sellers, the character actor best remembered as star of *The Goon Show* and the *Pink Panther* films, was born Richard Henry Sellers in Southsea, Portsmouth.

9 September 1513 – The Battle of Flodden. An invading Scottish army led by James IV of Scotland was defeated by an English army led by the Earl of Surrey on Flodden Field near Branxton, Northumberland. James IV was killed in the battle, the last monarch from the British Isles to suffer such a fate.

10 September 1547 – The Battle of Pinkie Cleugh, the last pitched battle between Scottish and English armies, was fought on the banks of the River Esk near Musselburgh.

11 September 1988 – Roger Hargreaves, the man who brought joy to millions of children with his Mr Men and Little Miss books and animated BBC television series, sadly passed away at the Kent and Sussex Hospital in Royal Tunbridge Wells.

12 September 1931 – Stage, screen and television actor Ian Holm was born in Goodmayes, Ilford.

13 September 1894 – J.B. Priestley, novelist, playwright and broadcaster best remembered for his 'Little Ships' broadcast after the Dunkirk evacuation in 1940, was born John Boynton Priestley in Bradford.

14 September 1852 – The Duke of Wellington, distinguished military commander, victor of the Battle of Waterloo and statesman, died at Walmer Castle, Kent.

15 September 1940 – Battle of Britain Day – A pivotal moment in the air war over Britain. The RAF, although fighting against superior numbers of the Luftwaffe, showed German High Command that air supremacy was not to be won easily, nor in a brief space of time and went a long way to convince them it may not be won at all. The threat of imminent invasion rapidly began to fade and Hitler shelved his immediate plans for invasion on 19 September.

16 September 1400 – Owain Glyndŵr was proclaimed Prince of Wales and raised the Welsh Revolt against the rule of Henry VI.

17 September 1929 – Motor racing legend Stirling Moss was born Stirling Craufurd Moss in London.

18 September 1879 – The Blackpool illuminations were switched on for the first time.

19 September 1356 – The Battle of Poitiers. An English army under the command of Edward, the Black Prince defeated a French army and captured the French king, Jean II.

20 September 1914 – Kenneth More, star of such films as *Reach for the Sky*, *Genevieve*, *The Battle of Britain* and *A Night to Remember* was born in Gerrards Cross, Buckinghamshire.

21 September 1745 – The Battle of Prestonpans. A Hanoverian army under the command of Sir John Cope was defeated – in ten minutes – by Jacobite forces under the command of Prince Charles Edward Stuart and Lord George Murray.

22 September 1791 – Scientist Michael Faraday, the man responsible for the discovery of the magnetic field, induction, diamagnetism and electrolysis was born in Newington Butts, Surrey.

23 September 1459 – The Battle of Blore Heath in Staffordshire, the first major battle of the Wars of the Roses, was a Yorkist victory.

24 September 1841 – The Sultan of Brunei ceded Sarawak to Great Britain and James Brooke became the first white Rajah.

25 September 1929 – Ronnie Barker, comedian and writer known for his roles in numerous British comedy television series was born Ronald William George Barker in Bedford.

26 September 1580 – Sir Francis Drake sailed his ship *Golden Hind* into Plymouth harbour and completed his circumnavigation of the world.

27 September 1825 – The Stockton & Darlington Railway was opened, becoming the world's first service of locomotive-hauled passenger trains.

28 September 1928 – Scottish biologist and pharmacologist Alexander Fleming noticed a bacteria-killing mould growing in his laboratory, a discovery that led to the development of penicillin.

29 September 1885 – The first practical public electric tramway in the world was opened from Cocker Street to Dean Street on Blackpool Promenade.

30 September 1967 – BBC Radio 1 was launched at 7.00 a.m. with Tony Blackburn presenting the first show.

OCTOBER

1 October 1847 – Women's rights activist and social campaigner Annie Besant, best remembered for her involvement in the Bryant & May's Match Girls' Strike of 1888, was born in Clapham, London.

2 October 1925 – Scottish engineer and inventor John Logie Baird achieved the first transmission of a television picture with a greyscale image.

3 October 1911 – Michael Hordern, distinguished stage and screen actor and narrator of the *Paddington Bear* stories was born at The Poplars, High Street, Berkhamstead.

4 October 1883 – The Boys' Brigade was established by William Alexander Smith at Free Church Mission Hall, North Woodside Road, Glasgow.

5 October 1930 – The British-built airship *R101* crashed in Beauvais, France, killing 46 of the 54 passengers instantly with a further two later dying in hospital. The bodies were all returned to England and were laid in state in Westminster Hall.

6 October 1854 – The Great Fire of Newcastle and Gateshead caused extensive damage, killed 53 and left hundreds injured.

7 October 1895 – End of the Cradley Heath (West Midlands) small-chain makers' strike after the majority of operatives were granted a 10 per cent wage increase.

8 October 1829 – Robert Stephenson's innovative steam locomotive *The Rocket* won the Rainhill Trials.

9 October 1936 – Big, bold and bearded character actor Brian Blessed was born in Mexborough, Doncaster.

10 October 1923 – Nicholas Parsons, host of classic 1970s quiz show *Sale of the Century* and chairman of BBC Radio 4's *Just a Minute*, was born Christopher Nicholas Parsons in Grantham, Lincolnshire.

11 October 1928 – The Tyne Bridge that links the city of Newcastle with the town of Gateshead was opened by King George V and Queen Mary, who were the first to use the roadway, travelling in their Ascot landau.

12 October 1872 – Ralph Vaughan Williams, composer and collector of English folk music and songs, was born at Down Ampney, Gloucestershire.

13 October 1884 – Greenwich was established as the Universal Time meridian of longitude.

14 October 1927 – Roger Moore, best known for his portrayals of 007 James Bond, Simon Templar in *The Saint* and Lord Brett Sinclair in *The Persuaders*, was born in Stockwell, London.

15 October 1881 – The quintessential English novelist P.G. Wodehouse, the creator of the *Jeeves and Wooster* books, was born Pelham Grenville Woodhouse at Guildford in Surrey.

16 October 1958 – BBC children's programme *Blue Peter* was broadcast for the first time.

17 October 1662 – King Charles II sells Dunkirk to Louis XIV King of France for 5,000,000 livres.

18 October 1016 – The Battle of Assandune. Fought between the armies of Canute the Dane and Edmund Ironside in Essex.

19 October 1858 – Allan Glaiser Minns was born in the Bahamas. Minns studied at Guy's Hospital in London and became the Medical Officer at Thetford Workhouse and for Thetford Cottage Hospital in Norfolk. He was elected Mayor of the Borough of Thetford in 1904 and with this appointment became Britain's first black mayor.

20 October 1827 – The Battle of Navarino was the last major naval battle fought entirely with sailing ships. A combined Ottoman and Egyptian armada was defeated by a British, French, and Russian naval force in Navarino Bay, Greece.

21 October 1805 – Admiral Lord Horatio Nelson was mortally wounded and died shortly after his victory was known at The Battle of Trafalgar.

22 October 1707 – The Scilly naval disaster. Four Royal Navy ships ran aground near the Isles of Scilly in a severe storm. Admiral Sir Cloudesley Shovell and over 1,400 sailors drowned.

23 October 1642 – The Battle of Edgehill, Warwickshire, was the first pitched battle of the English Civil War.

24 October 1882 – Distinguished British actress Dame Sybil Thorndike was born Agnes Sybil Thorndike in Gainsborough, Lincolnshire.

25 October 1415 – King Henry V led his English and Welsh forces to victory over the French at the Battle of Agincourt. On this same day in 1854 the Charge of the Light Brigade took place during the Battle of Balaclava.

26 October 1640 – The Treaty of Ripon was signed, restoring peace between Scotland and Charles I of England but its terms were humiliating to the king.

27 October 1939 – Comedian, actor and writer John Cleese, best known as a member of the Monty Python team and as Basil Fawlty in the classic BBC comedy *Fawlty Towers*, was born in Weston-super-Mare.

28 October 1903 – Evelyn Waugh, author of such classics as *Decline and Fall* (1928), *Scoop* (1938) and *Brideshead Revisited* (1945), was born Evelyn Arthur St John Waugh at 11 Hillfield Road, Hampstead, London.

29 October 1618 – Sir Walter Raleigh, soldier, spy, explorer and the man who popularised tobacco in England, was beheaded in the Old Palace Yard at the Palace of Westminster.

30 October 1960 – The first successful kidney transplant in the United Kingdom was performed by Michael Woodruff at the Edinburgh Royal Infirmary.

31 October 1620 – English diarist John Evelyn was born in Wotton, Surrey.

NOVEMBER

1 November 1611 – William Shakespeare's play *The Tempest* was performed for the first time by the King's Men at Whitehall Palace, London.

2 November 1936 – The British Broadcasting Corporation initiated the BBC Television Service.

3 November 1783 – A highwayman named John Austin was the last person to be hanged upon the notorious Tyburn Gallows in Middlesex (today, the site of the gallows is marked a short distance from Marble Arch).

4 November 1847 – Scottish physician James Young Simpson discovered the practical anaesthetic properties of chloroform.

5 November 1605 – Guy Fawkes was discovered under the Palace of Westminster and the 'Gunpowder plot' to blow up the House of Lords during the State Opening of Parliament was prevented.

6 November 1951 – The English gentleman actor Nigel Havers was born in London.

7 November 1665 – The *London Gazette* was first published as the *Oxford Gazette*.

8 November 1602 – The revived Oxford University Library reopened with generous support from former Merton fellow Thomas Bodley. Officially known as Bodley's Library, it is popularly referred to as the Bodleian Library and is one of the oldest libraries in Europe.

9 November 1907 – The Cullinan Diamond, the largest polished diamond in the world at the time, was presented by the Transvaal government to King Edward VII on his birthday.

10 November 1925 – Richard Burton, once the highest paid actor in Hollywood, famed for his performances in such films as *Who's Afraid of Virginia Woolf?*, *Anne of a Thousand Days*, *Equus* and *Where Eagles Dare*, was born Richard Walter Jenkins at Pontrhydyfen.

11 November 1918 – The Armistice brought an end to hostilities in the First World War. On this same day in 1920 the Unknown Soldier was buried in Westminster Abbey.

12 November 1944 – In Operation Catechism the German battleship *Tirpitz* was struck by a force of 32 Lancasters from Nos 9 and 617 Squadrons of the Royal Air Force.

13 November 1850 – Robert Louis Stevenson author of such classics as *Treasure Island* (1883), *Kidnapped* (1886) and *The Strange Case of Dr Jekyll and Mr Hyde* (1886), was born at 8 Howard Place, Edinburgh.

14 November 1922 – The first daily radio service was launched by the British Broadcasting Company.

15 November 1983 – English actor John Le Mesurier, affectionately remembered for his portrayal of the gentlemanly Sergeant Arthur Wilson in *Dad's Army*, passed away at his Ramsgate home. He wrote his own notice of his death which he left instructions to appear in *The Times*: 'John le Mesurier wishes it to be known that he had conked out on November 15th. He sadly misses his family and friends.'

16 November 1907 – RMS *Mauretania*, the sister ship of RMS *Lusitania*, set out on her maiden voyage from Liverpool to New York.

17 November 1887 – Field Marshal Bernard Law Montgomery, commander of the 'Desert Rats' of the 8th Army, victor of the Battle of El Alamein (1942), commander of Allied ground forces during Operation Overlord (1944), commander of the 21 Army Group for the liberation of North Western Europe and the man who took the German surrender in 1945, was born in Kennington, London.

18 November 1851 – The people of Aberdeen were fascinated by the demonstrations of 'the mysterious science of animal magnetism' and mesmerism demonstrated by Mr Lewis, 'a gentleman of colour'.

19 November 1919 – Alan Young, best known as the straight man to the talking horse Mr Ed in the American television show of the same name, was born Angus Young in North Shields, Northumberland.

20 November 1739 – A British fleet under Admiral Vernon secured a victory over the Spanish at the Battle of Porto Bello during the War of Jenkins' Ear.

21 November 1894 – Max Miller, 'The Cheeky Chappie', Britain's leading comedian of the 1930s, '40s and early '50s, was born Thomas Henry Sargent at Kemptown, Brighton.

22 November 1869 – *Cutty Sark*, one of the last tea clippers to be built, was launched at Dumbarton.

23 November 1963 – *Doctor Who* first appeared on BBC television.

24 November 1542 – The Battle of Solway Moss. A Scottish army under Lord Robert Maxwell was beaten by an English army led by Sir Thomas Wharton.

25 November 1952 – Agatha Christie's murder-mystery play *The Mousetrap* opened at the Ambassadors Theatre in London. Transferring to St Martin's Theatre in 1974, its run continues to this day and has the distinction of being the longest-running theatre production of the modern age.

26 November 1805 – The 1,007ft long Pontcysyllte Aqueduct, the longest and highest aqueduct in Britain, built by Thomas Telford and William Jessop, was opened on this day.

27 November 1925 – Ernie Wise, comedian and one half of the comedy duo Morecambe and Wise, was born Ernest Wiseman at Bramley, West Riding of Yorkshire.

28 November 1660 – The Royal Society of London for Improving Natural Knowledge, now known simply as the Royal Society, was formed.

29 November 1773 – Mr Foster Powell, an attorney's clerk, commenced a journey from London to York and back again on foot; a feat which he accomplished in the space of six days, reaching York on the Wednesday evening, and starting again the following morning for London, where he arrived on the evening of Saturday 4 December and bagged 100 guineas for achieving this extraordinary feat of pedestrianism.

30 November 1874 – Winston Churchill was born two months prematurely at Blenheim Palace, Woodstock, Oxfordshire.

DECEMBER

1 December 1919 – Nancy Astor became the first female Member of Parliament to take her seat in the House of Commons.

2 December 1872 – It was announced that experiments at the Central Telegraph Station in London had allowed as many as 90 messages to be transmitted in a single hour along the same wire between London and Southampton.

3 December 1753 – Samuel Crompton, the inventor of the 'Spinning Mule' that revolutionised the British textile industry, was born at Firwood Fold, Bolton.

4 December 1930 – Ronnie Corbett, actor, comedian and one half of The Two Ronnies (the other being Ronnie Barker), was born in Edinburgh.

5 December 1766 – Auctioneer James Christie conducted his first sale in London.

6 December 1768 – The first edition of the *Encyclopædia Britannica* was published in three volumes in Edinburgh by Andrew Bell and Colin Macfarquhar.

7 December 1732 – The Theatre Royal opened at Covent Garden, London. The first performance was William Congreve's *The Way of the World*.

8 December 1914 – A Royal Navy squadron under the command of Vice Admiral Doveton Sturdee defeated an inferior squadron of the Imperial German High Seas Fleet at the Battle of the Falkland Islands in the South Atlantic.

9 December 1934 – Much loved British stage and screen actress Judi Dench was born in Heworth, York.

10 December 1868 – The first traffic lights were installed outside the Palace of Westminster in London. Resembling railway signals, they used semaphore arms and were illuminated at night by red and green gas lamps.

11 December 1917 – The victorious General Edmund Allenby entered Jerusalem on foot out of respect for the Holy City.

12 December 1949 – Versatile actor Bill Nighy, a stalwart of brilliant British comedy and drama on film and television was born in Caterham, Surrey.

13 December 1643 – A victory for the Parliamentary forces at the Battle of Alton in Hampshire.

14 December 1896 – The Glasgow District Subway was opened.

15 December 1906 – The official opening of the Great Northern, Piccadilly & Brompton Railway by David Lloyd George, President of the Board of Trade.

16 December 1775 – Jane Austen, author of such classics as *Sense and Sensibility*, *Pride and Prejudice* and *Emma,* was born at Steventon Rectory, Hampshire.

17 December 1945 – Jacqueline Wilson, the author of the Tracy Beaker books was born in Bath.

18 December 1912 – Charles Dawson announced the discovery of Piltdown Man, a previously unknown early human at the Geological Society of London. It was later exposed as a hoax.

19 December 1902 – Distinguished English stage and screen actor Ralph Richardson was born on Tivoli Road, Cheltenham.

20 December 2007 – Elizabeth II became the oldest ever monarch of the United Kingdom, surpassing Queen Victoria, who lived for 81 years, 7 months and 29 days.

21 December 1844 – The Rochdale Society of Equitable Pioneers opened their Co-op, the first to pay a patronage dividend and provide a prototype adopted by all future co-operative societies in Britain.

22 December 1888 – British film producer J. Arthur Rank, founder of the Rank Organisation, was born Joseph Arthur Rank at Kingston upon Hull.

23 December 1688 – The Glorious Revolution – King James II fled to Paris after being deposed in favour of his nephew, William of Orange and his daughter Mary. James was received by his cousin and ally, Louis XIV, who offered him a palace and a pension.

24 December 1914 – The unofficial 'Christmas Truce' between the opposing British and German forces began spontaneously at a number of locations on the Western Front during the First World War and football was played in No Man's Land on Christmas Day.

25 December 1932 – The first Christmas message radio broadcast was made by King George V, but few realised it was written by Rudyard Kipling.

26 December 1959 – The first charity walk took place, along Icknield Way, in aid of the World Refugee Fund.

27 December 1904 – Premiere of J.M. Barrie's play *Peter Pan* at the Duke of York's Theatre, London.

28 December 1934 – Doyenne of British stage, film and television, Dame Maggie Smith was born in Ilford, London.

29 December 1809 – William Ewart Gladstone, Liberal statesman and man who served four separate terms as Prime Minister (more than any other person) was born at 62, Rodney Street, Liverpool.

30 December 1865 – Rudyard Kipling, best remembered as the author of that most British of poems 'If', the *Just So Stories* and *The Jungle Book*, was born in the Bombay Presidency of British India.

31 December 1960 – The farthing ceased to be legal tender in Great Britain.

ACKNOWLEDGEMENTS

Any attempt at a bibliography for this book would result in a very unwieldy list of publications, but the author would like to extend his thanks to his team of experts and friends who have made suggestions for subjects and facts to research and include, helped check facts and endured his obsession with and excitement for the strange and the obscure:

Ian Pycroft, Kitty Jones, Andrew Selwyn-Crome, Stewart P. Evans, Major Graham Bandy, Janet McBride, James Nice, Martin Sercombe, Britta Pollmuller, Martin and Pip Faulks, Rebecca Matthews, Kerry and Paul Nicholls, Richard Knight, Dr Stephen Cherry, Dr Vic Morgan, Theo Fanthorpe, Robert 'Bookman' Wright, Matt Simons, Heidi Reeve, Amanda Dyer, Marcus Jones, Sarah Stockdale, Helen Henry, Michael Howroyd, Julia and Nigel Gant, Daisy Robinson, Ken Besfor, Jenny Phillips, Sophie Dunn, Michelle Bullivant, Steve and Eve Bacon, Victoria Barrett, Adrian Vaughan, Dave King, Christine and David Parmenter, Robin Housego, the late John Timpson, my darling Molly and son Lawrence.